As a husband, daddy, papa prayer in each of those areas. Rhett's effective model reminds me to address each role and situation I may encounter, thereby accessing the protection and power promised by my fervent and effectual prayers.

—DAN MILLER
New York Times Bestselling Author of *48 Days to the Work – and Life – You Love*
Career Coach and Host of the popular *48 Days Podcast*

I first met Rhett Wilson when he was a young college student just getting ready to begin his seminary studies. A church member told me about this promising young man, and I was compelled to call him, and invite him to come and talk with me. Since that time God has used him in mighty ways. He is now a pastor, an author, an editor, a husband, and a father.

I was delighted when Rhett asked me to write an endorsement for this book. *The Seven Ps of Prayer* is a groundbreaking and easy to read book. We all need to pray for our families. However, many people do not pray simply because they do not know what to say. Rhett outlines the *7 Ps of Prayer* and makes it easy for parents and grandparents to pray daily for their families.

With all of the sin and violence surrounding our children on a daily basis, we must cover them in prayer. This book is a necessity for parents in our world today.

Rhett has also written a children's book titled, *Praying with Daddy,* using the same seven Ps of prayer. What a treasure.

—DR. DON WILTON
Pastor to Billy Graham; author of *Saturdays with Billy: My Friendship with Billy Graham*
Senior Pastor of First Baptist Spartanburg, South Carolina, 1993-2022
Board of Directors, Billy Graham Evangelistic Association

Thank you for the opportunity of endorsing your first book, *The 7 Ps of Prayer: A Simple Method to Pray for Your Family*, a daily method under 7 germane topics, you developed more than 10 years ago to pray for your children. What an amazing example with practical helps for readers!

Dr. Rhett Wilson, our friend and co-laborer in the Gospel, adroitly deals in this compelling work with the two primary factors of foundational family ministry. Since creation, *the family*, which is increasingly under consistent attack from every side by evil forces, and *prayer*, which is the indomitable power that pierces darkness and overcomes difficulties for one's family.

Rhett has shared in this encouraging and practical work, utilizing scripture, memorable stories from the present and salient quotes from the past, all organized by reader-friendly chapters, in a fashion that allows for daily impact on family life and worship. I highly recommend this work to anyone who wants to know the basics and intricacies of praying for and with one's family.

I have already commended this work to one family who has found themselves struggling at the moment — to read and organically digest together step by step to comprehend "how to" build up, heal, and strengthen each other and their family unit, receiving the blessings of Jesus' loving touch and the peace.

—DR. TOM PHILLIPS
Senior Advisor, Billy Graham Evangelistic Association

I've known Rhett for most of his life — and mine. He was a freshman in high school when I became his youth minister, but I watched him grow up as a young child. His love for God's Word, His people, and the call God has placed on his life push him onward even to this day. I have called on Rhett consistently over the years to contribute to both devotionals and magazines, and his writing is never found lacking. It's a ministry to those of us who are fortunate to read his work. Now, I call on you to take the time to hear this family man's heart in this timely book on prayer. I've witnessed Rhett pray for peace, God's purposes, God's plans, purity, provision, the Lord's presence, and protection. In *The 7 Ps of Prayer*, Rhett offers a simple and straightforward way for all of us to pray these same things for those nearest to our hearts.

—DAVID BENNETT
Managing Editor, *HomeLife* and *Open Windows*,
Lifeway Christian Resources

A salute to my friend Rhett Wilson, and his insightful encouragement about prayer - and the family. Praying is a profound and joyous connection in heart, life and purpose with the Creator of the Universe and the guardian of our souls. And yet, for many believers and more churches than we dare to count - prayer is a neglected ministry in the body of Christ. Without prayer - our preaching, our evangelism efforts, and our mission posture and programing are limited, and our families often disabled without power and distinct purpose. But, in prayerful connections - God works through His people and in our families. Rhett has provided a specific route for understanding, incorporating and engaging in the spiritual dimension of intercessory prayer for our families. A journey that may well change your heart, and the eternal direction for your family. I challenge you to read this work and put into practice these principles. When you do, there will be "joy" in the journey for your family – and spiritual strength for what lies ahead in life.

—DAVID BRUCE
Executive Vice-President, Billy Graham Evangelistic Association

Rhett is an outstanding writer who has learned how to capture the different voices we have at Leighton Ford Ministries. I love so much of what he produces. That's why I'm excited to recommend his book on praying for your family. He has a fresh word for people who want to see the blessing of God come down upon their families, children, grandchildren, and loved ones. I strongly encourage you to pick up a copy today!

—KEVIN GRAHAM FORD
Chief Catalyst, Leighton Ford Ministries
Author of *Transforming Church* and *The Leadership Triangle*
Chief architect of the *Transforming Church*
Insight congregational survey

When it comes to investing, there is no greater return on your effort than God's exponential favor on those for whom you pray. In The 7 Ps of Prayer, Dr. Rhett Wilson uses creative storytelling and Biblical insights to inspire and equip readers to pray consistently and intentionally for the next generation. If you have children or grandchildren, now or in the future, this book will help you invest spiritually in their lives for their eternal good and God's glory.

—LEE WEEKS
Assistant Editor of Decision Magazine
Co-author of *Turn Your Season Around: How God Transforms
Your Life,* the autobiography of Darryl Strawberry

Dr. Rhett Wilson, Sr., knows how important prayer is. *The 7 Ps of Prayer* reminds us of 7 words that can serve as a guide for our prayers. His system encourages you to develop a prayer plan to help you stay on track as you pray for your family. Intertwining personal stories and Scripture, you will learn how to develop a prayer plan that will leave you with a word for every day instead of sitting and wondering what you should be praying for.

—LINDA GILDEN
Carolina Christian Writers Conference Director
Best-selling and award-winning author, speaker, editor, writing and speaking coach, author of almost 50 books and over a thousand articles.

It is with the highest of recommendations that I endorse Dr. Wilson's book, *The Seven Ps of Prayer*. This book contains a strategic, yet simple plan of prayer that is both transformational and protective. Transformational in the sense that as God answers the prayers, it will lead to the lives of our children and grandchildren being transformed into the "image of Christ," as found in Romans 8:29. It is protective in the sense that the prayer is "standing in the gap and making up the hedge."

Since Dr. Wilson shared these principles and pattern of prayer, it has changed my prayer life, in regards to praying for my daughter and son-in-law and our four grandsons. I pray most days using Dr. Wilson's strategy and concept and I have seen God move in the lives of my daughter, son-in-law and four grandsons, in powerful and transformative ways. God is both honoring and answering prayers using this strategy.

—Dr. Joe T. Youngblood
Director of Missions, Moriah Baptist Association
President, Revival and Missions International

THE 7 Ps
of
PRAYER

A Simple Method to Pray for Your Family

DR. RHETT WILSON, SR.

END GAME
Press

7 Ps of Prayer: A Simple Method to Pray for Your Family

End Game Press books may be purchased in bulk at special discounts for sales promotion, corporate gifts, ministry, fund-raising, or educational purposes. Special editions can also be created to specifications. For details, contact Special Sales Dept., End Game Press, P.O. Box 206, Nesbit, MS 38651 or info@endgamepress.com.

Visit our website at www.endgamepress.com.

Library of Congress Control Number: 2023930751
Hardback ISBN: 978-1-63797-086-7
Paperback ISBN: 978-1-63797-105-5
eBook ISBN: 978-1-63797-087-4

Cover Design by Dan Pitts
Interior Design by Typewriter Creative Co.

Printed in India
10 9 8 7 6 5 4 3 2 1

In memory and honor of those who prayed much for me:

Janice G. Clark

Virginia G. Hendrix

Frances J. Hendrix

Morris "Moose" Keller

Marian H. Wilson

Eva Ann Via

And to Tracey Alane, a gift of love to me
I'm thankful for you and our Wilson Five.

"May His peace rest, His blessing be ours,

To radiate His glory in our union.

And may our home be filled with children,

God's grace and understanding.

And may our lives be marked by the love of Jesus."

—From the song, "One Flesh," written by Rhett
and sung to Tracey at our wedding in 1998

ACKNOWLEDGEMENTS

This book has been a dream of mine for more than a decade, since I first attended the Blue Ridge Mountains Christian Writers Conference. I want to thank Victoria Duerstock and her excellent team at End Game Press for seeing the vision for this project. Thanks to my agent, Del Duduit, for making the connections.

I appreciate the diligent work of my editor, Andrea Merrell, who is a pleasure to work with.

People who really pray for you are rare gifts. I've been amply blessed to link arms with believers who practiced a ministry of prayer and prayed earnestly for me and my family – more than I can name here. I'm especially mindful of some praying women in Clinton, South Carolina, who taught me much about intercession and conversational prayer. I remember with joy Alma "Mama G" Galloway, Nell Haggart, Sandy Brooks, and Emily Campbell. Thank you for praying – remembering that Jesus is in the room – and teaching others to pray.

TABLE OF CONTENTS

INTRODUCTION

The *pop-pop-pop* of gunfire put every muscle in Bruce Schmidt's body on high alert.

Bruce was painfully aware that people who lived in the Northern Ugandan bush country periodically raided the village where he and his family lived as missionaries. Hearing the sounds, Bruce knew they were under attack. He grabbed his six-year-old son and threw him on the floor. Spreading his body over his child, Bruce prayed, "Father, I cannot keep a bullet from hitting my son. But if it is going to hit him, it is going to have to go through me first." Thankfully, the Schmidts experienced protection from the raiders. In the process, Bruce modeled how a parent can protect his or her family.

Although we may not face the same kind of attack, the enemy comes today to attack our families, churches, and nation. We can't stop him from coming. We can't immunize our families from attacks. We can't control other people's decisions. Nor can we keep the evil one's fiery darts from flying. But another option exists. Dads and moms, grandmas and grandpas can lift up a shield of prayer. We can cover our families and those we love with the habit of a praying life. We can give our wives, children, and grandchildren the heritage of prayer. At the end of the day, we can pray, "Father, I cannot keep the enemy from attacking my family, but he will first have to go through my prayers."

Jesus wants to bless our homes. The family is the basic building block of society, and the home is the first place God wants to give His glory and blessings. Matthew Henry said that if "our houses be houses of the Lord, we shall for that reason love home."[i] Today, more than ever, we need our houses to be houses of the Lord.

Jesus described His people in Mark 11:17 as a house of prayer. What is God's house? We are. The Bible says, *"Do you not know that you are God's temple and that God's Spirit dwells in you?"* (1 Corinthians 3:17, English Standard Version). The Living Bible says it this way: *"God's home is holy and clean, and you are that home."*

The Bible doesn't call believers God's temple because they meet in a building with a steeple. The building only holds the real church, the people, for a few hours weekly. As the people come together, they make up the house of God, whether they meet in a home, restaurant, or park. Jesus said when His people gather, they become a house of prayer (Mark 11:17). God desires a people marked by the breath of prayer. He savors His bride ornamented by the atmosphere and environment of prayer.

I'm thrilled to journey with you on one of the greatest adventures a person can take—learning how to strategically, passionately, and purposefully lift up a shield of prayer over our families and loved ones. We can influence our children, grandchildren, churches, and generations to come.

Covered

"How do I clean this up before my wife gets out of the bathroom?" I quickly thought. It was Black Friday morning, the day after Thanksgiving in 2001, and our little family of three was enjoying a quiet morning at home before going shopping that afternoon.

Tracey and I were young parents of our one-year-old son. While Tracey showered, Hendrix and I played on the floor in my bedroom. Not yet walking, though he could stand, he would scoot around the house with lightning speed. He crawled out of our bedroom, across the hall, and into our kitchen.

In less than one minute, I heard curious sounds coming from the other room—the kind of sounds a young child makes when he discovers something new and unfamiliar. I promise he was not out of my sight for more than sixty seconds. Hearing his sounds, I investigated. I crawled into the hall and popped my head around the door jamb. What a sight awaited me.

Tracey and I had recently painted a child's rocking chair a bold, barn red. We left one quart of paint on a low shelf in the kitchen. Low enough for a baby to reach. Note to young parents—put the paint higher.

In less than sixty seconds, our adorable baby boy crawled into the kitchen, found the can of paint, turned it upside down, and poured out all of the contents. Engraved in my memory is Hendrix sitting cross-legged in a pool of paint wearing only a diaper and onesie, completely drenched in barn-red paint from his waist down.

After the immediate shock, I did what any strong, able-bodied man would do in the same situation. I thought, "How in the world do I clean this all up before Tracey gets out of the shower?"

I sprung into action. First, I grabbed him up, taking him outside. Now, in those kinds of situations you don't exactly think through much. You just do the next thing. It was about forty-five degrees outside. Being a stellar father, I plopped a near-naked Hendrix down onto the cold driveway. When his bare feet hit the drive, he raised his hands, gave me a hard look, and started screaming. Again, I showed great Daddy wisdom. As he stood and yelled, I ran back inside. In retrospect, I'm glad our across-the-street neighbor didn't witness the scene. With a toddler drenched in red from his belly-down, it probably looked like blood, and the neighbor might have called the police.

In a flash, I ran to our second bathroom, grabbed towels and mopped up the paint in the kitchen. Then I grabbed a big towel, ran outside, and scooped up Hendrix, who was still yelling at me.

Hurrying to the back of the house, I turned on the bathwater and quickly bathed him. Thankfully, the paint was water-based and not oil-based, or we might still be scrubbing. In what I thought was an amazing feat, I cleaned up Hendrix, with my boy wearing a fresh diaper and onesie, and the house before ever seeing my wife.

When she did emerge ready for the day, she immediately asked, "What have you guys been doing?" Well, it made for quite a story.

As long as we lived there, little baby, red footprints marked the driveway right next to the side door of our house.

Remembering how Hendrix literally covered himself with paint, I've often reflected how I need the Lord to cover me. The Bible says about the red blood of Jesus Christ, *"With his own blood ... he entered the Most Holy Place once for all time and secured our redemption forever"* (Hebrews 9:12, New Living Translation). The author of Hebrews goes on to say because of His death, *"Jesus opened a new and life-giving way"* with direct access to the presence of God (Hebrews 10:20a, NLT). He covered me with His blood, securing my eternal future.

I need the Lord to cover all of me. He is my hiding place (Psalm 32:7), and I dwell in the Almighty's shadow (Psalm 91:1). I need Him to shield, cloak, and canopy my family and those for whom I pray.

Seven Words to Pray for My Family is about asking God to cover us —all of us—so that He can have His way and that *"our sons in their youth will be like plants full grown, our daughters like corner pillars cut for the structure of a palace"* (Psalm 144:12, ESV).

A Pleasant Smell

Prayer is like incense, a pleasant aroma to the Lord. My family loves Yankee Candles. Once, on a family vacation to Williamsburg, Virginia, we visited the Yankee Candle Village. Candle lovers could enjoy over 400,000 candles in over two hundred scents. We like to give these candles as gifts, and we like to receive them. Sitting at my desk, I can imagine the calming, pleasing effect of walking into our house when a Yankee Candle burns. The scent of Blueberry Scones, Salted Caramel, Balsam and Cedar—or my favorite, Apple Pumpkin—makes stepping into the home inviting.

The Bible gives various descriptions for prayer. One found in Revelation 8:3-4 describes prayer as incense. When God hears our prayers, it's like He's sitting on the throne experiencing the wonderful scent of his favorite Yankee Candle wafting up to His presence. The psalmist prayed, *"May my prayer be set before you like incense; may the lifting up of my hands be like the evening sacrifice"* (Psalm 141:2, NIV).

Prayer Shield

Because we can run our lives, families, and churches with little prayer, too many people try to function without a prayer covering. The American church exists in a land of plenty. We store food in pantries, money in banks, and an abundance of clothes in closets. Our garages overflow with items that could go to a thrift store. We make our plans and ask Him to bless them. Because of our relative comfort and prosperity, we may function without a dynamic daily dependence on the Lord. However, Jesus desires that we pray to Him for our daily bread.

Donald Whitney, professor of Spiritual Formation at The Southern Baptist Theological Seminary, writes:

> The contemporary church has technology, psychology, and marketing, but do we know anything about the power of God upon our preaching and ministry? The Bible and

the testimony of church history say that, despite how out-dated it may seem, the effectiveness of the gospel and of the church are inseparably related to the united prayers of God's people.[ii]

The church operates at its best when her people pray togeth-er regularly. Yes, we should work, give, and meet needs. We can serve others through our spiritual gifts and sacrifices. But our work can't do what the power of God can.

Unfortunately, in most American churches, the pastor's Bi-ble study has replaced the weekly prayer meeting, or prayer is relegated to reading a list of sick folks and having the pastor pray for about three minutes before he teaches. John Frank-lin wrote a book to pastors called *And the Place Was Shaken: How to Lead a Powerful Prayer Meeting*. Several years ago, I attended a one-day seminar that Franklin led at First Baptist, Woodstock, Georgia, about making prayer the main item in a church's prayer meeting. It was one of the most powerful training events I've ever attended. Franklin shares that gener-ally, North American churches "have abandoned fervent, unit-ed, corporate prayer," and "until we return to this practice, we should expect to see continuing decline in societal morals and an increase in powerless churches."[iii]

Families thirst for that divine touch. We raise our children in a society that has embraced immorality and moral relativ-ism. Public shootings occur much too frequently. A spirit of cynicism and criticism hangs over our culture. Our teens see a sex-crazed entertainment industry rejecting biblical stan-dards. The public educational system has largely discarded the Bible as irrelevant. Illegitimate births have increased over 300 percent.

With these and other land mines facing moms and dads, our families need the Lord to do what only He can do. The world needs houses of prayer—individuals, families, and churches—taking up that mantle and operating in the atmosphere of intercession.

Nehemiah's Gates

The story of Nehemiah takes place after the Babylonian captivity. For seventy years, the Jewish captives lived away from their homeland. In 539 BC, Cyrus the Great of Persia issued a decree and released them, allowing the Jews to go home and begin a new life. Under Governor Zerubbabel, the remnant returned and rebuilt the temple. But the walls lay in waste, making the families of Jerusalem vulnerable to constant attack. Ancient cities depended on their walls for protection. The effectiveness of the borders depended on the all-important gate. People knew that in warfare, an unsecure gate left the wall and city defenseless. If an enemy broke through the gate, the opposing army could penetrate the city.

My family enjoys watching *The Lord of the Rings* movie trilogy. In several battles of Middle Earth, intense fighting scenes occur at walled cities. In *The Two Towers,* the plot builds to the Battle of Helm's Deep. Theoden, King of Rohan, and his forces attempt to protect the fortress from the intruding Uruk-hai orcs. These fierce creatures of war arrive with massive ladders and catapults. Their strategy? Breach the gates and penetrate the wall. The forty-minute movie-battle, considered one of the greatest ever filmed, reaches a climax when the orcs devise a way to breach the gates by using a medieval explosive. Once they puncture them, the city soon falls.

Although *The Lord of the Rings* is fiction, the life of Nehemiah was not. A godly and prayerful man, he understood the necessity of building the walls and securing the gates. Under God's direction, he led the people to rebuild. Upon completion, they celebrated with thanksgiving and singing. Bible scholars believe the people may have sung Psalm 147 at the wall's dedication (Nehemiah 12:27). The people praised God for rebuilt walls and restored gates, thus fortifying the peace and security within for the people.

As a father, I want to provide security for my family. For years, we purchased season passes at Dollywood. Well, actually, my three children did not purchase them. I did. I spent about $125 for each child to have a season pass. With those passes, we experienced the thrill of riding the wooden roller-coaster (the Thunderhead in Timber Canyon), flew on America's first wing roller coaster (The Wild Eagle), enjoyed outstanding shows with singing and dancing, and ate until our bellies were full at Aunt Granny's Buffet. My family enjoyed those benefits because I bought those perks. With me comes certain blessings.

This passage in Psalm 147 describes the blessings accompanying the Lord's protection. Seven benefits result when the Lord is our wall:

- *Building Up* (vs. 2) – He is able to construct things in our life for our benefit.

- *Binding and Healing* (vs. 3) – He takes the broken pieces of our life and repairs them. He puts His balm on our heart wounds, bringing restoration.
- *Lifting* (vs. 6) – God finds afflicted, fallen people and lifts them back onto their feet again.
- *Providing* (vs. 9, 14) – The Lord sustains us and replenishes our material supply.
- *Strengthening* (vs. 13) – Though we use natural methods and means to protect our lives and families, only God's ultimate blessing keeps us secure.
- *Blessing* (vs. 13) – We want the Lord's favor on our lives. He places His supernatural hand of abundance on our children and grandchildren.
- *Making Peace* (vs. 14) – No lasting peace exists apart from the Prince of Peace. God gives us one of life's greatest blessings—peace.

In ancient times, a person entered or left the city only through the gates—openings in the walls. The strength of the gates depended completely upon the bars. These large, strong beams of wood lay horizontally across the gate's middle section. The ends were inserted into iron hooks or clamps which attached to the city's stone walls. Nehemiah 3 shows the builders setting the doors, bolts, and bars of the wall (3:3, 6, 13-15). A strong, secure bar produced a firm and fastened gate.[iv] A gate without strong bars left the walls unprotected. The city would immediately become unsecure once an enemy permeated the gate.

The Bar of the Fear of the Lord

When I use my spiritual imagination, I see two bars for the

gates in Psalm 147. The first bar needed for our family's stability is the **fear of the Lord** (vs. 10-11). Fearing the Lord means to have a deep respect for Him, His ways, and His Word. When Dr. Luke wrote the book of Acts, he characterized the church in Judea, Galilee, and Samaria as living *"in the fear of the Lord"* (Acts 9:31). When individuals, families, and churches walk in the fear of God, they invite His blessing. They invite His protection, watch, care, and peace.

The Bar of Praise and Worship

The **power of praise and worship** is a second symbolic bar for our life's gate. When we set ourselves to worship the Lord, praising Him for His attributes, we welcome God's activity.

In spite of our troubles, sorrows, or obstacles, praise lifts our eyes to the Lord, who is able to handle every circumstance in our lives. Not only does praising the Lord help us mentally and psychologically, it opens the door for the Spirit of God to empower us.

Darlene Deibler Rose served as a missionary in the interior of New Guinea. During World War II, she spent four years in Kampili, a Japanese forced-labor prison camp. Dealing with the malnutrition, isolation, and interrogations that accompanied life on that island resulted in enormous hurt and stress. Darlene learned to worship and praise the Lord in her cell, which became her sanctuary. She recited Bible verses memorized in her childhood, recalled the words of hymns, and poured out her heart to the Lord.

One day she discovered a knife hidden on the window sill of her cell. Terrified the guards would find the weapon and incriminate her, she later wrote:

Then, on my knees with my face to the floor, I explained the whole hopelessness of the situation to the Lord. With the telling, quietness invaded my spirit, and I began to worship the God of Abraham, Isaac, and Jacob, the God of Elijah and Daniel, the God of miracles. "Lord, if you could open the Red Sea to deliver Your people from Egyptian tyranny, and if You could send Your angel to shut the mouths of lions that they might not kill Daniel—then, Lord, it is nothing to You to remove that knife. Thank You, Father."[v]

She never left her cell for three days. Late in the third day, she looked again on the ledge to find the knife gone. Reflecting on this event, Darlene said, "What I needed to do was link my impotence to God's omnipotence."[vi]

The power of praising the Lord lifted her spirits from her prison into His presence.

The Enemy of Our Homes

Every generation throughout time has faced temptations and a battle with the flesh. Our nature always wants to resist God and His truth. In the lives recorded in the book of Genesis, we read of murder, hatred, lust, rape, incest, arrogance, selfishness, deception, cover-up, drunkenness, slavery, and sibling rivalry, just to name a few problems. There is nothing new under the sun. History is filled with cycles of morality and immorality, downward spirals, reforms and revivals. And in every new day, people must decide to either go their own way or *"call upon the name of the LORD"* (Genesis 4:26b, ESV).

The Bible describes the Devil as a thief who wants to steal, kill, and destroy us and our families (John 10:10). He wants to damage our children and grandchildren. But be aware that his attacks and infiltration may come subtly.

In the tale of the Trojan Horse, after a ten-year siege, the Greeks failed to penetrate the city of Troy due to the fortified walls. Devising a clever plan, they pretended to sail away, leaving a large wooden horse at the city's gate. The Trojans mistook it as a gift and pulled the monstrosity inside. During the middle of the night, the soldiers hidden inside the horse quietly crept outside and opened the city's gates for the rest of the Grecian army to enter. The Greeks conquered Troy and ended the war.

Today, the term Trojan Horse refers to a program that appears harmless but, once allowed into a computer's system, wreaks havoc. While claiming to rid your system of viruses, a Trojan adds destructive ones.

Satan and evil want to subtly and secretly worm their way into your family, creating trouble and heartache. The Trojans experienced defeat because the enemy infiltrated their gates. Today, our enemy does not possess unlimited access to us and our families unless we leave the gates open through prayerlessness and neglect. Bruce Schmidt understood the power of the wall and the gate. He realized he was the wall and gate for his son. He declared, "Father, if evil is going to touch my son, it must first go through me."

Unguarded Homes and Ungated Lives

Many people today have unguarded homes and ungated lives. How does this happen? It starts with a hurried life. James Dobson, Christian psychologist and founder of Focus on the

Family, warns the greatest threat to the health of the family in the Western world is not drugs, gambling, or immorality. The greatest danger is the busy pace of society. If we do not fight against that constant frantic pace, it leads to an always-hurried life. A hurried life finds little time for prayer, Bible meditation, and instructing our sons and daughters in the things of the Lord. A Finnish proverb says, "God did not create hurry."

James Dobson says, "Crowded lives produce fatigue—and fatigue produces irritability—and irritability produces indifference—and indifference can be interpreted by the child as a lack of genuine affection and personal esteem."[vii]

For thousands of years, the world existed without electricity. When the sun set, people slowed down. Families spent time together in the kitchen or den. They talked, played music, shared ideas, and read books together by candlelight. Christian families read the Bible and prayed. And they went to bed and slept full nights. When darkness came, it was almost time for bed.

A little more than a century ago, things significantly changed. With electricity, suddenly the average household could manipulate light, providing the means and motivation to go to sleep later. Then, somewhat sadly, during the 1950s, the television became the centerpiece of the average American household. In our age, with the coming of internet technology, people can constantly be connected to endless amounts of information and entertainment. But we are paying the price. Sleep deprivation has become normative in our society. Many families never sit down for a meal together without the interruption of the television or smart phones. Families spend less time engaging in meaningful conversations, reading substantive material, and enjoying each other compared to previous generations.

My twenty-one-year-old says, "I wish people still sat on their porches after supper, played music, talked, and just enjoyed being together." When was the last time your family read a book together out loud? Or read from the Bible together? Or sat around the table in an unhurried fashion and discussed ideas? We are wise to glean lessons from the days prior to electricity and modern advancements.

An unguarded life results from an always-hurried one. We become willing to let things go that we normally would not. We neglect habits that on better days we deem necessary. We delay important activities, setting them aside day after day and week after week. We go days without spending time with the Lord, without meaningful conversations with our spouse and children, without calling our parents or grandparents, without having uninterrupted time around the family table. Before we realize it, we watch and listen to entertainment that normally we avoid. We tune in to smart phones more than concentrating on relationships. Our attitudes and habits grow lazy. Our lips become loose, and we choose practices we previously avoided.

Life becomes unguarded, and an unguarded life leads to a proud one. A proud person thinks, *I can handle this. I know how to do this. I know how to run my life, family, and church. We are doing pretty well just like we are.* And a proud life will eventually become a sinful one.

Dads and moms, grandmas and grandpas, we can guard our lives and gate our homes. We can take up the responsibility of praying for those under our influence. We can be houses of prayer.

The 7 Ps

Several years ago, as a young father with preschool-age children, I realized my awesome responsibility to pray for them. Struck with the reality that no other man would pray for my children more than me, I asked God to help me design a simple but comprehensive strategy. A tool to help me guard our lives and gate the walls. That search produced what I call *The 7 Ps of Prayer: Seven Words to Pray for My Family.* Each day of the week includes a corresponding word beginning with the letter *P* to pray for one aspect of my family's life and needs. I have used this guide for years to pray for my wife and children, and now that my children are teenagers, I continue to pray the 7 Ps.

In the following pages, I will teach you seven words that can transform your prayer life as you stand in the gap for your family. And you will read real-life stories of answered prayer from parents and grandparents I know personally.

As I have prayed for my own family through the years, the 7 Ps have become a natural part of my prayer life:

- Monday – Pray for peace.
- Tuesday – Pray for God's purposes.
- Wednesday – Pray for God's plans.
- Thursday – Pray for purity.
- Friday – Pray for provision.

- Saturday – Pray for the Lord's presence.
- Sunday – Pray for protection.

The enemy, trouble, and temptations will come. Will they find we left the gate open through neglect? Or will we throw ourselves shamelessly over our family in prayer saying, "It has to go through me first"? Together, let's boldly declare, "We stand at the gate of our city, and we will not leave the gate open through prayerlessness."

Sunshine Magazine once included the comment, "Don't expect a thousand-dollar answer to a ten-cent prayer."[viii] Join me as together we learn how to build strong walls for the sake of our families, praying for God to do great and amazing things.

Week One: Called to Peace

A Testimony of Peace

"We screamed. We cried. We begged. But the choice had to be hers."

My cousin Cary Strange and his wife Heather live in Lawrenceville, Georgia, with their five children. A few years ago, they endured a trial with their daughter Hannah. At age nine, she struggled with anxiety and became afraid of vomiting. She decided that not eating would take care of that problem.

Hannah would eat a tiny breakfast and lunch and later announce she was so full she did not need supper. Heather said, "Almost every night became a battle. We pleaded with her. We tried to reason with her. We explained the health benefits and risks. We threatened to sit on her and force-feed her."

Hannah lost a lot of weight. At her smallest, she weighed forty-nine pounds. Her stomach hurt all the time. Her skin sank into her ribs. The bones in her back protruded. Dark circles surfaced around her eyes. A sad, lethargic spirit came over her. The family's pediatrician told Hannah that if she did not eat, she would eventually die.

During this time, Cary and Heather received advice from many people who loved them. Numerous folks pleaded with them to seek more professional help from psychiatrists. Heather shared, "As my husband and I prayed through this, neither of us had peace about that route. We don't have a problem with the medical world, so it did not make sense to me that we did not feel right about pursuing help. Every fiber of my being wanted to fix her fast. But there was an unmistakable, quiet answer in our spirit that said, *Wait.*"

After a confrontation with a well-meaning loved one pleading with her to get outside help, Heather replied, "This is bigger than either of us. But it is not bigger than the Lord. He created her. He knows what it will take to defeat this. He alone can set her free."

The next morning, Heather seemed to reach a breaking point. Pleading with the Lord in her prayer time, she remembered the words of the song "Mighty to Save."[ix] That mother rehearsed the truth back to the Lord for her child that if He can move a mountain, He can move a nine-year-old to eat.

Finally, Cary decided to fast and pray for ten days. During that time, he went without food and drank only water. With every hunger pang came the reminder to pray for Hannah. Cary drew his strength from the Lord. He dove into the Scriptures with an unquenchable desire to seek Him for wisdom, protection, and healing for his first-born baby girl.

A few days later, as Heather prepared one of the family's

favorite meals, tacos, she prayed fervently that the Lord would go ahead of them that night at supper.

Hannah entered the room and asked, "What's for supper tonight?"

Heather calmly replied, "Taco ring." Heather waited, feeling like she was pouring sweat. The mother never looked up for fear of her emotions running wild. She waited for the excuses of why Hannah would not eat. Heather desperately cried, *"Please, Lord, please,"* as she stood there mixing the ingredients in the bowl. Then she heard a bewildered, 'Huh?'"

Hannah walked over to the utensil drawer and took out a spoon. She dipped into the taco bowl and ate a very large spoonful of taco meat. Heather almost fell on the floor. Still, she was quiet, trying to act normal.

Hannah took two more bites and looked at her mother in shock and joy. Then she exclaimed, "Mommy! I'm not afraid to eat tonight. I'm not afraid!"

Hannah danced around the kitchen island singing, "Jesus answered my prayers. I've been set free. Jesus answered my prayers. I've been set free. I'm not afraid. He's set me free!"

At this point, Heather was bawling in the kitchen. At that very moment, she witnessed her nine-year-old daughter delivered from oppression. Together they felt the chains drop and experienced freedom. According to Heather, "Hannah felt the weight that had been her constant companion lift and disappear."

Hannah returned to normal eating habits for a growing girl. Her weight and physical qualities soon returned to a healthy appearance. At age twelve, Hannah told her mother one day,

"Mommy, eating is my new hobby. I love to eat." Today, as I write, Hannah is a productive college student.

Heather said, "I felt such a surge of peace, joy, and excitement. God gave me a gift to remind me of His faithfulness."

Peace returned to the Strange family.

Peaceful Homes

Everyone wants to live in a peaceful home. No one wants to live in a family marked by unrest and turmoil. Discussing the home, the apostle Paul reminded the Corinthians, *"God has called us to live in peace"* (1 Corinthians 7:15b, NIV).

One sad reality of today's society is the absence of peace. When my kids were little, I loved tucking them into bed at night. My wife and I flip-flopped with our children. One night she took our daughter and the next night our sons, and vice-versa. Our sons shared a room, which included a cool bunkbed with a double bed on the bottom. I spent hours on that bottom bed lying next to my boys, telling stories, laughing, and listening.

Peace matters. I wanted my children to wake up in the morning and lie down at night in a home marked by peace. I remember one of those routine nights when I put my boys to bed in their fun pirate bedsheets and comforters. The three of us lay together on the bottom bunk for an extended amount of time. The conversation turned spiritual, and my youngest son asked specific questions about opening his life to the Lord. My oldest son was already a Christian, and the two of us talked with Dawson about what it means to become a believer. Finally, Dawson said, "I want to pray right now for

Jesus Christ to come into my life." Hendrix, Dawson, and I got onto our knees in their bedroom. We all prayed together, and for the first time, Dawson opened the door of his heart to Jesus Christ.

An interesting promise appears in the book of Isaiah: *"The result of righteousness will be peace; the effect of righteousness will be quiet confidence forever. Then my people will dwell in a peaceful place, in safe and secure dwellings"* (32:17-18, CSB). For years, I asked the Lord to make that true of my family.

Many people search for peace. But the peace *of* God starts by having peace *with* God. And peace with God comes only through trusting what Jesus Christ did on the cross as the payment in full for our sins and then by inviting Him personally to come into our hearts, yielding the throne of our lives to Him.

As I learned to pray for my children, I began the practice of praying the word *peace* for them every Monday.

Shalom

Shalom is one of those cool, fancy Bible words—a traditional Jewish greeting used to wish someone God's best. The English language translates shalom as peace. In Old Testament times, peace meant "completeness, soundness, and well-being of the total person."[x]

The *Names of God Bible* explains: "In its deepest meaning, it expressed the hope that the person you are greeting may be well in every sense of the word—fulfilled, satisfied, prosperous, healthy, and in harmony with themselves, others, and God."[xi]

We first encounter this name of God in the Old Testament

account of Gideon. Located in the book of Judges, we find God's people in trouble because they neglected the Lord. To humble them, God had allowed the Midianites to oppress them for seven years. The result was a lot of hardship and cruelty. The Bible describes the Midianites as *"thick as locusts,"* coming in at harvest time, devouring and destroying their crops *"until the land was stripped bare"* (Judges 6:5,6, NLT).

Enter Gideon. We find this young man threshing wheat at the bottom of a winepress at his daddy's place in Ophrah. In biblical days, the bottom of a winepress was not a good place to thresh wheat.

At harvest time, after collecting stalks of grain from the fields, people gathered at the threshing floor—a flattened out-door surface usually made of wood or stone. They laid their harvest on the floor where cattle or oxen walked across it. This process crushed and broke the sheaves, separating the grain from the husks. This specific step is called *threshing.* Then, workers tossed the grain into the air, allowing the wind to blow away the chaff and letting the edible part fall on the floor. Workers built threshing floors on open plains to allow for plenty of wind to make the process easier. The community gathered there at harvest time and made it a group event.[xii]

So why is Gideon threshing wheat at the bottom of a wine-press dug into the ground for people to walk on grapes? Gideon fears. He hides. He can't go out in the open to the threshing floor because the Midianites might see him. So, he's doing it incognito at home. And he's alone. There's no harvest party, no community coming together for hard work and camaraderie. It's just our man Gideon. And it probably indicates a small harvest.

What he didn't know is that, in response to the cries of His people, God is about to do a great thing. He sends the angel of the Lord to sit beside the great tree at Ophrah, which belonged to Gideon's father, Joash. And here God's Word reveals several reasons Gideon needs God's peace. And you know what? Human nature and God's truths have not changed. In these verses in Judges 6, we also find reasons that you and I need peace. We'll explore them in the coming weeks.

Questions to Consider

1. Why do you think the Lord places such value on peace in our home?
2. Do you know the peace of God that only comes from having peace with God?
3. Where do you need the Shalom of God in your life and family?

Prayers for this Week

Father, may we live in such a way that invites Your peace into our home.

If you want to skip to week one of Purposes, head to page 65.

Week Two: The Lord is With You

When Facing an Enemy

Israel had good reason to be afraid. The cruelty of the Midianites forced the Israelites to make *"hiding places for themselves in the mountains, caves, and strongholds"* (Judges 6:2, NLT). They faced massive enemy hordes who *"arrived on droves of camels too numerous to count"* (Judges 6:5, NLT)).

Today, Christians in America face enemies. Ask Russell Vought. During the 2017 confirmation hearing for the deputy White House budget director, Sen. Bernie Sanders questioned Vought on his theological beliefs about Muslims. Because Vought once defended Wheaton University for firing a professor who believed that Christians and Muslims serve the same God, Senator Sanders kept questioning him about his theological convictions on salvation. When Vought responded with "the centrality of Jesus Christ in salvation," explaining he was a Christian and Christians historically believe the Bible says that Christ is necessary for salvation, Sen. Sanders answered, "I would simply say, Mr. Chairman, that this nominee is really not someone who this country is supposed to be about." There is intolerance on full display.

Your enemy may be an ungodly family member, an unruly neighbor, or a boss or co-worker who seems to have it in for you.

When Life is Hard and We're Doing All We Know to Do

Gideon found himself in a tough spot. Though at first the picture of the young man hiding in the winepress may seem pathetic, it also shows a noble trait. During a difficult time, he did everything he knew to do. The book of Proverbs says, *"If you do nothing in a difficult time, your strength is limited"* (24:10, CSB). Gideon didn't know how to solve the entire problem for his people or his family. But he could go to the winepress and thresh wheat for their immediate needs.

One quality of a godly man is that he simply does what needs to be done. No fanfare. No selfies on social media. Just roll up the sleeves and do it. We have tried, even though not always successfully, to teach our children to have this approach at home. If you see the trash can is full, empty it. If the dishwasher is full of clean dishes, unload it. If the towels are dry, fold them.

When facing enemies, we can become so overwhelmed by the magnitude of the problem that fear tells us to do nothing. Fear and anxiety want to immobilize us so that during a difficult time we sit on our hands instead of taking action. But the

Bible says, *"the people who know their God will display strength and take action"* (Daniel 11:32, NASB).

Several years ago, my wife and I walked through a new and unexpected trial. The small church I pastored struggled financially, and my wife and I knew we needed another source of income. After months of praying, getting counsel, and exploring options, we began a slow transition of my resigning from the church, relocating to my hometown, and beginning a training program with a financial planning firm. I studied intensely for five weeks under their program. Financial advisors must pass several comprehensive exams to be certified. Some financial companies allow their new employees to take those tests several times. This particular company requires new hirees to take the hardest test first. When I took it the first time, I did not score high enough for the company. Their human resources representative called me and in three minutes said they were "beginning the process of separation," and that I was off the payroll immediately. In less time than it takes to walk to my mailbox, life threw a curveball. After changing jobs, putting our house on the market, and making significant changes to pursue this career, suddenly, the game board shifted.

I told my wife, "We are going to choose to see this transition as coming from God. It surprised us, but it did not surprise Him. We are not going to live in fear. The Lord is our source, and He is going to care for us."

Transitions come at us suddenly. The change may be in job or income. Variations may come through illness, death, divorce, or the loss of friendship. Though we rarely anticipate

such switches, they come nonetheless. After working and sup-
porting my family for almost twenty years, we never saw it
coming. I thought, *I'm not the kind of person who gets fired.
I'm responsible. I've kept jobs and supported my family for two
decades.* During that season, our enemies loomed large. *How
will we make it? Where will I work? How will we provide for
three teenagers without a full-time job?*

A man losing his job can be one of the most traumatic experiences of his life. During that time in my own life, a man
from another city who heard about me called and took me out
to lunch. He had lost his job several years earlier and walked
through similar waters. He looked at me over lunch at Ruby
Tuesday and said, "Losing my job was the hardest thing I have
ever gone through in my life."

Early in the process, I realized I could not control how,
when, or where I got another job. And I could not do anything about the past. I had two general choices in front of
me. I could become a couch potato, binge-watch Netflix, gain
weight, and become depressed. Or I could see the extra time
on my hands as a blessing and use it to delve into motivational
reading material, freelance writing, and job-hunting. I chose
the latter. I read and listened to a lot of positive, helpful books
by authors like Andy Andrews, Mark Batterson, and Dan
Miller. I devoured Steve Farrar's book *Manna: When You're
Out of Options, God Will Provide.* I probably read something
from his book every day I was unemployed. Then, instead of
filling my mind with useless hours of entertainment, I saw
the extra time as a gift to work on my writing. And I began a
thorough job search. Using Dan Miller's *48 Days to the Work*

You Love, I learned how to better understand my skills, values, traits, and passions; how to organize them into a strengths-based resume; and how to communicate those characteristics succinctly and effectively.

No, I couldn't control when I got the next job. But I could control what I did each day.

In those months, I took the time to begin developing my own freelance writing and editing business. And, after being a stay-at-home homeschool mom for eighteen years, my wife searched for employment. She eventually began working as a secretary at a CPA firm. No, it wasn't ideal. And we hoped it would not last for long, but it was something concrete she could do at the present.

We couldn't see the big picture. We didn't know how it would end. Sometimes we feared we might crash and burn. But in those times, when you are doing everything you know to do, you need peace from God that He holds your big picture together.

When We Feel Abandoned

The angel told Gideon, *"Mighty hero, the Lord is with you!"* (Judges 6:12, NLT).

Gideon responded, *"Sir, if the Lord is with us, why has all this happened to us?"* (Judges 6:13, NIV). In other words, he felt abandoned. He's saying, "Life is tough. Things are hard. My people are starving and scared. They're hiding in caves, leaving their homes. We don't know what to do, and we don't know when God will help us."

I felt that way at times during my unemployment. When

the bills stacked up. When God seemed silent. When friends didn't come around. One of the big surprises for me when I lost my job was how few of my friends reached out to me. I guess I expected a lot of phone calls, emails, and invitations to lunch from brothers trying to build me up. But I can count on one hand the men who made an effort to check on me and motivate me. I did have one dear lady in our church who loved us and understood our situation. For several months, I received a check from her with an encouraging word. But during those months I remember feeling very alone. It was Martin Luther King, Jr., who said, "In the end, we will remember not the words of our enemies, but the silence of our friends."

My advice if you have a friend who loses a job? Do three things.

One, pray for them.

Two, contact them regularly during the unemployment, at least monthly. That means at the bare minimum a phone call, email, or text. Better yet, take them out to eat and encourage them.

And third? Send them some money. They probably need it, and it likely won't embarrass them. They have bills to pay, and they will be thankful you care enough about them during this time to think practically.

And don't ignore them. It may make you uncomfortable because you don't know what to say, but remember that Paul told us, *"Share each other's burdens, and in this way obey the law of Christ"* (Galatians 6:2, NLT). Your friend will be glad you remembered him when he was down.

Ultimately, though, the follower of Christ learns to lean on the Lord, who is always near. When trouble comes, it's one thing to call our friends, send out emails, and post on social media. But the Lord wants us to learn to go to Him as our source. We can say confidently, "The LORD is my helper," and "Even if my father and mother abandon me, the LORD will hold me close" (Hebrews 13:6; Psalm 27:10 NLT).

Questions to Consider

1. What obstacle in your life currently feels like an enemy standing in your way?
2. How can you take action even in a difficult situation you currently face?
3. Who in your life is going through a trial that may need your encouragement?

Prayer for this Week

Father, thank You that even in my darkest days, You do not abandon me. Enable me to remember who You are, rest in Your promises, and lean on Your everlasting arms. May Your peace be a mark of my life and family.

If you want to skip to week two of Purposes, head to page 73.

Week Three: Surprises

When God Surprises Us

The Lord had plans for Gideon and Israel (and the Midianites, by the way). The angel of the Lord, whom scholars believe was actually an Old Testament appearance of the Lord Jesus Christ, turned to Gideon and said, *"Go with the strength you have, and rescue Israel from the Midianites. I am sending you!"* (Judges 6:14, NLT). A new opportunity arose in Gideon's life. He didn't expect it. He didn't plan for it. And he did not see it coming. But it came. And it surprised him.

Life's redirections can keep us sensitive, pliable, and moldable to the Lord. The difficulties we encounter shape our character and lead us to consider paths and opportunities we previously ignored. During our season of transition, my wife received an unexpected call. The worship director at her home church resigned, and they wondered if she would consider doing the interim part-time. Her parents lived two hours from us, but she could commute for a few months on Sundays and Wednesdays. Tracey was a church music major in college and led music in a volunteer or part-time basis at several of our churches through the years. We saw it as a short-term provision and a good way for her to spend time with her parents. I told her when she started, "After you do this for about two weeks, they are going to want you to do it full-time." The people loved her and responded wonderfully to her leadership. And sure enough, in a few weeks, they asked if she would consider coming full-time as their Minister of Worship.

A new opportunity arose for us. One we had never considered. For twenty years, we lived away from her family and never thought we would have an option to live close to them. But you never know with God.

Suddenly, Tracey and I had a whole new set of circumstances in front of us. After praying and discussing it for a few months, we agreed for her to take the job, and our family relocated to Lancaster, South Carolina. It was a difficult transition, but one with new blessings. For two years, we lived three doors down from her parents. My children could ride their bikes or take a walk down to Pop and Meemie's house after school or on weekends. We never thought we'd live near her family, and for a season we enjoyed walking distance. And, surprisingly, within less than nine months I accepted the position of Senior Writer for the Billy Graham Evangelistic Association in Charlotte, North Carolina, within driving distance of Lancaster. Our foresight could never have shown us I'd be writing for the President's office of one of the world's largest and most influential Christian organizations.

Abraham walked with God into new places (see Hebrews 11:8). My youth pastor once exhorted, "Rhett, if you can ever tell me exactly what you will be doing six months from now, you are no longer walking by faith." That nugget of advice has stayed with me for twenty-eight years.

Following God, according to Eugene Peterson, becomes a "long obedience in the same direction."[xiii]

When We're Unsure

Trying to process everything going on, Gideon lacked reassurance. He heard what the angel said, but it seemed impossible. It didn't make sense. And it was way beyond his natural ability and visible resources.

I believe Gideon gets a bad rap for what he does next. In his uncertainty, he played a game with God. Two different times, he asked for a sign. Before you throw this book across the room and call me a heretic, let me say that I don't believe the Bible teaches that it is normative to ask for signs.

Gideon boldly asked, *"If you are truly going to help me, show me a sign to prove that it is really the Lord speaking to me"* (Judges 6:17. NLT). Gideon prepared a meal offering, bringing meat in a basket and broth in a pot, and presented them to the angel. In response to the angelic being, he placed the meat on a rock and poured the broth over it.

I remember needing peace one time when I was unsure. During my college years, I dated a young lady off and on for about three years. As often happens with dating couples their senior year of college, the question loomed large, *Are we going to get married, or are we just enjoying each other's company as college students?*

We talked and prayed about marriage. She was a serious Christian, an exciting person, and I thought she would make a good wife and mother. We shared similar goals. From the world's perspective, and even from the vantage point of many believers, we probably could have experienced a better-than-average marriage.

But going into the last semester of my senior year, a nagging lack of peace accompanied my thoughts of her. This finally culminated in a decision in February when I told her I was sure God was not leading us to be married. It was a somewhat sudden change and surprise to her, but I believed God answered our prayers for direction. After college we parted ways.

Pastor Don Wilton of First Baptist, Spartanburg, South Carolina, shares advice for counseling pre-married couples. He does not ask them, "Do you know that it is God's will for you to marry each other?" That question can be manipulated because of strong emotional attachment. He asks instead, "Do you know that if you did not marry this person, you would be out of God's will?" That is much stronger.

More than a year after college graduation, I still had no future marriage prospects. Several of my friends were married or engaged, and it felt like the clock was ticking. My mother suggested I reconsider my college girlfriend, but I knew the Lord had closed that door. Over several months, however, I did begin to consider another young woman. Without question, I wanted a wife who was a serious Christ-follower. The woman I considered certainly was. In fact, I could not think of any woman I knew who was more serious in her relationship with God.

I finally bit the bullet and wrote her a lengthy letter. Thankfully, email was just getting started, and we resorted to snail-mail (which is still a great idea for weighty matters). I laid it out, told her she was the kind of woman I hoped to marry, and asked her to pray about whether we might have a future. I mailed the letter in early autumn and waited. And waited.

Weeks and months rolled on, and before long it was January of 1997. After taking a semester off from school, I moved back to Louisville, Kentucky, to re-enroll in seminary. The first day in my dorm room, I asked the Lord to give me a word from Scripture to cling to in the coming weeks, one that would be a milepost for that new season of life. On January 4, I wrote down Isaiah 42:16 in my journal:

> *I will lead the blind by ways they have not known, along unfamiliar paths I will guide them; I will turn the darkness into light before them and make the rough places smooth. These are the things I will do; I will not forsake them* (NIV).

For three weeks I memorized and meditated on that promise, trusting God to fulfill it. The weekend of January 26, I visited my uncle in Cincinnati, Ohio. On Sunday morning, walking into the Sunday school room at their church, I noticed a bright orange banner along the wall with Isaiah 50:7 (NIV) painted across it: *"Because the Sovereign Lord helps me, I will not be disgraced. Therefore have I set my face like flint, and I know I will not be put to shame."*

The Lord put a check in my spirit at that moment. A check occurs when the Holy Spirit alerts you on the inside as if to say, "Listen up. I am speaking. I have something for you here." I made a mental note of the Bible verse and also wrote it down.

That night I drove along Interstate 71 back to Louisville, pondering those two verses. Isaiah 42:16 promised divine guidance. In other words, *I can trust my steps to Him.* The other verse in Isaiah spoke of not being put to shame. I internalized that as, *God will not shame me. I don't have to be afraid. He has my best interests at heart.*

Arriving on campus, I checked my mailbox. Inside was a note from the girl I wrote in the fall. Walking across the chilly campus to Whitsitt Hall, I prayed, *Lord, whatever this holds, I commit the outcome to you.* Sitting down on my blue love seat in the small dorm room, I read the letter. She kindly and respectfully turned me down and said she did not think we had a future together. She also told me, "Since I received your letter in the fall, I have been praying two Bible verses for you: Isaiah 42:16 and Isaiah 50:7."

I was stunned. The refusal from the young lady did not phase me. It was one of those moments when you feel like, *Well, this is not what is best for me, so thank God.* It was the reality of how the Lord spoke through those specific verses that overwhelmed me. I later learned that such an experience is what Robert Clinton calls a "double word confirmation" in his book *The Making of a Leader.*

I walked across campus with my Bible to a grassy hill that looks out at the library. Time seemed to stand still as I sensed God's presence. Submitting my life to Him afresh, I asked the Lord to have His way with me in the coming days.

That was Sunday night. It was one of the defining moments in my life.

On Friday night, I met the woman of my dreams—the one I would marry.

Tracey Funderburk moved to the campus of The Southern Baptist Theological Seminary that very week. Not knowing why she needed to attend the school but sensing the Lord's direction to enroll at SBTS, she moved 500 miles from Lancaster, South Carolina. We met that Friday night at a music school party.

Prior to leaving my dorm room for the party, I stretched out on the floor with my Bible and journal, asking the Lord to direct my steps. I wrote:

> Whatever is in the future, in the days ahead, Lord, I trust You. I want to abide in You and let you do through me whatever You want. To lead along new paths. Guide in ways I have not known. But You know it thoroughly, Father. So I am yours. I give myself to You. I walk into the unknown trusting as a child.

Two hours later, I returned to my small dormitory and penned: "I met a girl tonight—a new student. She went to North Greenville University and worked at Crossway Book Store. Tracey Funderburk. Wow. Psalm 37:4."

Twelve months later on a cold winter night, I asked her to marry me in the steeple of Alumni Chapel. Six months later we were married on a hot July afternoon.

Twenty-one years and three children later, the rest is history. God is able to be trusted with the details of our lives. He sees the total canvas, and as we only see the day to day, we rest in the watchcare of the One who is Sovereign over the seasons. I'm still thankful for the Unseen One who is able to lead us along unfamiliar paths and make rough places smooth.

Questions to Consider

1. What surprising redirection have you experienced, forcing you to trust God?
2. Consider that the Lord may be currently allowing you to face a closed door in order to get you to a different opportunity.
3. Where are you unsure and need God to make Himself known to you in your life? Don't be afraid to ask Him.

Prayer for this Week

Father, thank You for being the One who can lead me along unfamiliar paths, guiding me and my family. Where there is darkness, please turn it into light, and where there are rough places, make them smooth. I go forward trusting that You will never forsake us.

If you want to skip to week three of Purposes, head to page 81.

Week Four: Renewing and Maintaining

When We Are Afraid We Have Missed God

When Gideon brings a meal offering to the Lord's angel, the Bible says the angel touched it with his staff, and fire flamed up from the rock to consume the offering.

Gideon suddenly realized he was visited by an angel. Struck with the reality this stranger was God and not just a man, he feared his own death. The Lord graciously told him to not be afraid, and the young man responded in worship: *"And Gideon built an altar to the Lord there and named it Yahweh-Shalom (which means 'the Lord is peace')"* (Judges 6:24a, NLT). Later in the Bible, the prophets refer to Jesus Christ as the Prince of Peace. But here, Gideon calls God "Jehovah-Shalom," the God of Peace.

Through the years, I've learned how much I need His peace in my own decision-making. I tend to second-guess myself.

I wish I didn't. My wife has an amazing ability to forget a lot of bad things. I don't. I generally remember them. And if I'm not vigilant, especially with my melancholy temperament, I brood over them.

I'm also a recovering perfectionist. And sometimes it colors my practical theology. One Scripture helpful for people like me is Ecclesiastes 11:4, *"He who watches the wind [waiting for all conditions to be perfect] will not sow [seed], and he who looks at the clouds will not reap [a harvest]"* (AMP). In her book, *Do It Scared,* Ruth Soukup calls perfectionists procrastinators— not because we are lazy, but because we are afraid of making mistakes.

I can mentally trace back cause-and-effect scenarios from years ago and berate myself for not making better decisions. Sometimes my wife has to tell me, "Don't you know God is bigger than that? He can handle those things. He doesn't just have a plan for yesterday. He knew everything that would happen, and He has a plan for today."

Several times in my life I have feared I missed God. One of those times occurred years ago while working as an associate pastor at a church. The staff experienced a lot of internal conflict, and I found myself in a season where I felt unnoticed and used below my potential. We lived in a small town for a number of years, and I longed to be living in a more exciting urban area. I wondered if we had simply missed God.

One day while brooding in my spirit, I went to lunch at a local Mexican restaurant. Over chips, salsa, and chicken fajitas, I read some of Adrian Rogers's book *What Every Christian Ought to Know.* He says:

You say, "I missed it. When I was young, God had a plan for my life, and now that I'm old, I think … it's too late for me." It's never too late for you. God has a will for your life and every stage of your life … If you've had some years that you think were wasted, let God give you a fresh start.[xiv]

Christian discussion on living in God's will can fall into one of two extremes. One train of thought seems to place the emphasis on a believer discovering or finding God's will for their life. Inadvertently, this thinking creates some unnecessary anxiety: *What if I went to the wrong school, took the wrong job, or went to Burger King and was supposed to go to Wendy's?*

Another line of thinking says believers are simply to use their brains and ask God for wisdom. This path can ignore the place of God's Spirit giving specific guidance into an individual life or group.

Jerry Bridges' book *31 Days Toward Trusting God* helped me immensely several years ago when I was wading through my own questions about following God's will. I so appreciate his perspective on this subject:

> Like most Christians, I've struggled over the right choice at some of those "fork in the road" decision points we encounter from time to time. I may have made some wrong decisions; I don't know. But God in His sovereignty has faithfully guided me in His path through right decisions and wrong ones. I'm where I am today not because I've always made wise decisions or correctly discovered the will of God at particular points along the way but because God has faithfully led me and guided me along the path of His will for me.[xv]

Trusting God to guide us brings peace only He can offer. The key to walking in the peace of God is not mainly emotion or some mystical, feel-good encounter. The solution to experiencing God's Shalom is maintaining a disciplined mind.

Renewing

Romans 12:1-2 summarizes the prerequisite and process of spiritual growth. After writing about our great salvation for eleven chapters, Paul turns the page and exhorts the believer to surrender to God (vs. 1). But as I used to hear at youth camps as a teenager, the problem with a living sacrifice is that we want to crawl off the altar. So, Paul tells us a specific action to practice in order to keep walking in the spirit of surrender. That action? *Renew the mind.*

The scenario has played out for as long as youth groups have gone to camp. The entire week builds to the last night of camp—decision time. Speakers challenge teens to give their lives to Jesus, repent, and turn to Him. Hundreds of sincere teens respond saying, "I want to give up my bad habits of smoking, doing drugs, watching porn, and having sex. I want to live for Jesus this year." Unfortunately, for many—perhaps most of them—if you followed their lives a month down the road, you would find them right back into the same habits. Why? What happened? Sincerity wasn't the problem. And actually, surrender probably wasn't the problem. So, what was it?

Submission alone does not equal transformation. Surrendering to Jesus must be followed by the daily renewing of our minds. The mind is the battleground for the Christian life.

Actions, good and bad, start as thoughts. And thoughts can follow habits. Paul tells believers that to continue walking with God, controlling our minds is essential. I love how the Phillips translation says it: *"Don't let the world around you squeeze you into its own mold, but let God re-mold your minds from within, so that you may prove in practice that the plan of God for you is good, meets all his demands and moves towards the goal of true maturity."* (Romans 12:1, J.B. Phillips New Testament)

Walking in God's peace requires renewing the mind—actively putting God's Word into our mind daily. This includes removing some negative mental influences. Our lives are like boats with holes. Instead of spending our time pouring out water from the boat, we should spend time plugging up the holes. That's why if those teens return from youth camp and continue listening to the same ungodly, sensual, profanity-laced music and entertainment, the filthy water will continue pouring into their boats and affecting their lives.

The Christian life requires daily, regular, renewing of the mind with the Word of God.

Maintaining

Paul outlines the second prerequisite for walking in the peace of God in Philippians 4:4-9, which some people call the believer's prescription for mental health. Paul exhorts the Christians toward several actions:

- Choose to rejoice (vs. 4). We can choose our attitude.
- Practice the Lord's presence (vs. 5). Remember, He lives inside of you.

- Pray with thanksgiving (vs. 6). Habitually talk to God about your life. And add thanksgiving to it as an act of trust.
- Keep your mind focused on things in keeping with the Lord (vs. 8).
- And finally, don't just think about these things, but internalize them (vs. 9). Obey them.

The promise made by the apostle to the Philippians is one of the most wonderful ones in all of Scripture: *"And the peace of God, which surpasses all comprehension, will guard your hearts and your minds in Christ Jesus"* (Philippians 4:7, NASB). The word here pictures a military soldier standing guard. That's a promise we all need. But notice, for the peace of God to come, the believer must control his or her mind. Isaiah makes a similar claim in chapter 26:3.

On Mondays, pray for the peace of God to reign in your family.

Questions to Consider

1. Where do you feel like you have missed God? Ask Him to reassure you with His sovereign plan—even over your mistakes.
2. How do you need to rid yourself of negative input into your eyes and ears? What holes need plugging?
3. What can you practice this week to help you and your family maintain a focus on good, wholesome, positive material?

Prayer for this Week

Father, I'm reminded that the battle for life and victory starts in the mind. Help me to renew my mind daily, allowing Your truth and positive input to enable me to keep my focus on You and make right choices in life.

If you want to skip to week four of Purposes, head to page 89.

PRAYER POINTS FOR PEACE

As Gideon learned to walk in the reality of Jehovah-Shalom, so I want my family to walk in the reality of the Lord's peace. Here are five points to pray for the Prince of Peace to make Himself known in our lives:

1. Pray for them to have peace with God through salvation.
   - When we enter a relationship with God through His Son, the Bible says we have peace with God through Christ
   - As the bumper sticker says, *No God, no peace. Know God, know peace.*

2. Pray for them to experience God's peace by the nearness of His presence.
   - Asaph wrote, *"the nearness of God is my good"* (Psalm 73:28, NASB). The sense of His presence was and is a refuge for the believer.
   - Because the Lord is near, believers can choose to not be controlled by fear, anxiety, and a wavering spirit. With God's help and our self-control, we can exhibit strength and stability.
   - Charles Stanley says, "Our intimacy with God—His highest priority for our lives—determines the impact of our lives."[xvi]

3. Ask the Lord to help them develop a disciplined mind guarded by peace.
   - The Bible models the importance of having a sound mind focused on good, true, and godly ideas.

- The Bible tells us to let Christ's peace rule our hearts (Colossians 3:15). The idea is the role of an umpire in an athletic event. God's peace can guide believers in decision-making and godly living.

4. Pray for each family member to have homes marked by the Lord's peace.
   - See Isaiah 32:17-18.
   - God wants our homes marked by security, love, and wholeness.

5. Ask for God to raise them up as agents of the gospel of peace.
   - Jesus said, *"Blessed are the peacemakers, for they will be called children of God"* (Matthew 5:9, NIV).
   - As we practice the attitude of submission to one another in our relationships, we can make for peace.
   - Paul used the image of believers wearing the shoes of peace in battle: *"with your feet fitted with the readiness that comes from the gospel of peace"* (Ephesians 6:15 NIV). Because of the gospel, we have peace with God and can have confidence in life's battles with the nearness of our God. As we stand firm in Him, we can be ministers of that gospel of peace.

PRAYER FOR GOD'S PURPOSES

Week One: Waiting and Trusting

My long-time friend Cathy Schwartz allowed me to write her testimony of an amazing provision in the life of her family:

"Hey, honey, guess what happened to me today?" Jay asked as he walked in the door. "I got laid off."

"That's great!" I said, stunned to hear myself say these words to my husband.

Even though we didn't know how we would make ends meet, I wasn't worried. We'd been praying for God to bring a change in Jay's work, believing that would mean a new position or moving to another company. In spite of the fact this wasn't what we'd had in mind, I knew God owned the cattle on a thousand hills, and He could surely take care of our finances.

I was curious, however, as to how He would provide.

Jay was burned out from the stress of working seventy to eighty-hour weeks as an electrical-computer engineer, leaving little time for our two small children, Sally and Greg, and me. We missed him. We wanted out of our rut. So we began praying in May of 1992. On September 22 of the same year, Jay, a well-respected employee who'd made a positive difference in the company, lost his job due to outsourcing. They no longer needed him.

That day we embarked on a six-month journey of unemployment, relying only on a small weekly unemployment check to survive. Four of those checks added together were not enough to make our house payment, much less two car payments, and take care of two children ages five and eight who liked to eat. We had no idea how we would make it. But I kept reminding Jay, "God owns the cattle on a thousand hills, and He will take care of us."

We did fine through December. Anytime our checkbook got dangerously low, an anonymous cashier's check arrived in the mail. This drove our children crazy. "Mom," they'd beg, "we have to find out who is sending these checks."

"Sweeties," I'd say, "as far as I'm concerned, God drops them out of heaven into our mailbox." I know, of course, God didn't do that, but I do know He impressed others through His Holy Spirit to mail us those cashier's checks, and because of those checks, we never lacked any need. Our faith grew by leaps and bounds.

As December rolled into January, Jay was discouraged. It was difficult to be without work. Although he sent out numerous resumés and even tried unsuccessfully to start a company, he was not any closer to finding a job. When he was down, I'd lift him up, and he would do the same for me.

However, on January 9, 1993, we hit the bottom at the same time. Lamenting our circumstances, we cried out to

God, asking, "Why have you not provided another job? What are we doing wrong?" Followed by the biggest question of all, "Why are we faithfully giving away ten percent of our unemployment check to our church if You're not going to help us?"

Through the previous weeks, the Lord kept bringing one word to us through sermons, Scriptures, phone calls, and cards from friends. The instruction that kept coming was a nasty, four-letter word: wait.

I thought, *Well, I don't like to wait. It's not fun.*

We realized God was showing us that if we would wait on Him, He would pour out His blessings. So, as we prayed together that night, Jay prayed, "Lord, please forgive our impatience and lack of faith. Help us to continue trusting You as we wait."

After we prayed, I went to bed to read *His Mysterious Ways,* a book someone gave me for Christmas, which is a compilation of four hundred articles featured monthly in *Guideposts* magazine about how God worked in someone's life. Reading one each night helped strengthen my faith.

This night's story was from Eva Mae Ramsey, whose sister-in-law, Muriel, was sick with a diseased kidney. Eva and her husband drove for hours to be present during Muriel's surgery. On the way there, Eva felt impressed to take her sister-in-law one red rose. She found one in a shop near the hospital and put it in a vase next to Muriel's bed in the recovery room. Unfortunately, Eva Mae and her husband had to leave before they could talk to her after surgery. Soon after, though, they received a letter. In it, Muriel shared, "I prayed that if I was supposed to live, God would send me a sign I specifically asked for. When I opened my eyes after the operation, there it was, the very thing I'd prayed for—a red rose."[xvii]

Eva Mae couldn't have understood the significance of that gift when she obeyed the prompting. But God knew and sent her to bring one red rose as a sign of His watch care.

Putting the book on my bed, I looked up toward heaven and prayed, "Lord, I've never asked You for anything out of the ordinary before, but I need a reminder that You are here with me and are taking care of me and my family. Would You send me one long-stem red rose?"

After I prayed, I immediately fell asleep. I was careful not to tell anyone of my prayer, a little ashamed that I asked God for something so small after all He'd done to provide for us. But I needed some reassurance of His presence.

Ten days passed. I put that prayer out of my mind, thinking how foolish I was to ask God for such a thing.

Returning from taking my son to kindergarten, I stopped at a busy intersection where a Jiffy Lube sat on the corner. Suddenly, a distinct impression overcame me that I needed to go to the Jiffy Lube for an oil change.

Now, I'm faithful about getting my car to Jiffy Lube every 3,000 miles, but I'm also a penny pincher. The decal on the upper left corner of my windshield indicated I still had 800 miles to go before my next service. Even though the voice in my spirit repeated that I needed to go to the Jiffy Lube, I hesitated.

The light stayed red. I believe God held that light until I got over my stubbornness. Once again, I sensed in my spirit, *Go into Jiffy Lube and get your oil changed.* Even though I didn't understand why, I obeyed. Maybe God had someone in there He wanted me to meet.

I pulled my van into one of the bays and went inside. I frequented this Jiffy Lube many times before and after that day. But that day was different. In the past, lots of people crowded the waiting room—but not at that divine moment. Working behind the counter was a sweet older man. I love senior adults and worked for years in the senior adult ministry at church. Walking straight to the counter, I extended my hand to the man and said, "Hi, I'm Cathy Schwartz, who are you?" His name was Bob, and we hit it off immediately, enjoying a delightful conversation that seemed to include everything but Jay and his job situation. After about fifteen minutes my car was finished, and I paid Bob. As I walked toward the door and grabbed the handle, Bob said, "Mrs. Schwartz, come back here, I've got something for you."

Turning around, I saw Bob reach behind the counter and hand me a single, long-stem red rose. That is the only time I have known a Jiffy Lube to have a long-stem red rose behind the counter.

At that moment I could hardly breathe. When I prayed for the rose, I wasn't sure where it would come from. The Jiffy Lube man certainly was not in my top ten. I grabbed my rose without saying a word to Bob and ran to my car where I fell apart. I cried and praised God. Then I laughed and said, "God, You've got the greatest sense of humor. Never in my wildest dreams did I expect to get my rose from the Jiffy Lube man."

I hurried home to call Jay, who was somewhere making resumés. When I reached him, I excitedly poured out the whole story about my prayer. It lifted him completely out of the depths. God answered my prayer and affirmed He was still with me and my family.

Two months later, a company to which he had not even applied offered Jay a job. Now, more than twenty years later, he is still with that company, and God has blessed us beyond our wildest imagination.

There are two verses that sustained us during our layoff and still do today. *"And my God will supply all your needs according to His riches in glory by Christ Jesus"* (Philippians 4:19, NASB) and *"God is our refuge and strength, A very present help in trouble"* (Psalm 46:1, NASB).

When God sent me that rose, I knew I had to share my story. This led me to design a program that combined my testimony with the playing of musical instruments. My desire was not only to entertain, but also to inspire. Fittingly, I performed my first program for the senior adult group at my home church in Greenville, South Carolina.

After my first performance, I quickly discovered that if someone liked my program, she would tell her friend, who would tell her friend, and so on. The calls started coming in, and twenty-three years later I booked my 1,025th program of *Rose Petal Ministries.* I've had the privilege of performing in seven southeastern states as well as Indiana, Iowa, and Pennsylvania, playing the hammered dulcimer, piano, and hand bells while telling stories of God's faithfulness.

I'm still amazed how God used a prayer, a rose, and a Jiffy Lube employee to bring assurance to me. He really can be trusted to care for His own.

I wonder if you can relate to Jay and Cathy's story. We probably all know what it's like to walk through seasons of life where we face unexpected challenges and daunting obstacles. In those times, we may wonder, "Does God really see me?" Be encouraged from the testimony of the rose that you are not forgotten. The Lord knows your name. And He has a purpose for your life and family.

Questions to Consider

1. What present difficulty tempts you to run in fear rather than walk by faith?
2. Where in your family do you need to trust in God's provision—both now and in the future?
3. How can you remind your children or grandchildren that God has a purpose for their lives?

Prayer for this Week

Father, thank You for being our Creator and planning for our lives before the foundation of the world. Enable me to put my trust in You even when unexpected challenges rear their heads. Continue reminding me that You are intimately aware of me.

If you want to skip to week one of Plans, head to page 99.

Week Two: Fruit-Bearing

Our Creator

Gideon kept finding himself in situations that left him needing God's peace. As he discovered Jehovah-Shalom, he walked in the purposes and plans for his life. Those plans came from his Creator-God, also known as Elohim. The name first occurs in Genesis 1:1, which can be translated, *In the beginning, Elohim created the heavens and earth.* The Old Testament primarily translates it "God." Gideon's account refers to God as Elohim several times, including when Gideon asks God to prove Himself through a fleece at night.

Names are important. In the classic book, *How to Win Friends and Influence People,* Dale Carnegie taught that names are "the sweetest and most important sound in any language."[xviii] They identify an individual, calling them out from the crowd. They reveal importance.

We purposefully named our children. Our first born

received my name: Rhett Hendrix Wilson, Jr. Our daughter, Anna-Frances, was named partly after several important women in our lives all named Frances. Our third child, Dawson, was partly named after Dawson Trotman, the founder of the Navigators' disciple-making ministry.

The first day our son went to a four-year-old preschool class, the teacher gathered the children in a circle for everyone to share their names. She later told my wife that at Hendrix's turn, he said, "My name is Hendrix Wilson. My Mommy's name is Tracey Wilson. My Daddy's name is Rhett Wilson. And we have Anna-Frances." Yes, names do matter.

My sophomore year of college, I studied Kay Arthur's book *Lord, I Want to Know You.* She takes readers on an adventure to discover many of the Old Testament names of God. She writes: "You are the unique and distinctive handiwork of Elohim. Yes, He created the heavens and the earth. He formed the swirling galaxies ... But He also formed you. Specifically. Individually. Thoughtfully. Carefully."[xix]

Elohim had specific plans for Gideon. And that road involved lots of surprises requiring him to trust God.

Trusting God

When I was a boy, my great-aunt Frances sent several notes to me each year. Every time, she included one Bible passage: Proverbs 3:5-6. It says, *"Trust in the Lord with all your heart and lean not on your own understanding; in all your ways submit to him, and he will make your paths straight"* (NIV).

The Lord constantly teaches His people to trust Him. The entire Christian life is one continuous experience of trusting

God. And trusting God, shown through our obedience, allows God to maximize our influence.

On Purpose

Webster's New Dictionary defines *purpose* as an "intention, resolution, or determination."[xx] Did you know God has a purpose for our lives? Philosophers may spill vats of ink debating the subject, but one simple statement provides the answer: we exist to glorify God.

Jesus shed light on what it means to glorify Him. In John 15:8, He explained, *"By this my Father is glorified, that you bear much fruit and so prove to be my disciples"* (ESV).

Did you catch that? I love it when the Bible makes things simple. The Father receives glory today when you and I (a) bear much fruit and (b) show that we are really His disciples.

Bearing Fruit

There are only two ways I know to bear fruit: character and influence.

As we submit to the lordship of Christ and the authority of His Word, and as we learn to walk in the fullness of the Holy Spirit, the Lord gradually begins changing our character. Bad traits replace good ones. Our lives show the fruit of the Spirit, as outlined in Galatians 5:22-23, rather than the lusts of the flesh. Faithfulness becomes normal behavior. I'm not talking about perfection. I define faithfulness as a person going with God and walking with Him ninety percent of the time. Yes, this person occasionally takes his or her eyes off the Lord, gets fleshly, and sins, but quickly repents, gets back on track, and allows the Spirit of God to direct his or her life. As Proverbs 24:16a says, *"The godly may trip seven times, but they will get up again"* (NLT).

A person's bearing fruit influences others positively for Christ. The results will be as varied as the people in Christ's Body. Depending on your spiritual gifts, natural temperament, passions, and abilities, your reach will be unique. A writer in Zambia affects people differently than a businessman in Chicago. A farmer in Iowa experiences different results than an evangelist in Siberia. A doctor with the gift of mercy touches people in his community differently than a financial counselor with the gift of administration or a mother in her home caring for children. But nevertheless, as God has access to your life, you influence others.

What's the difference between bearing fruit and producing fruit? When I was a sophomore in college, I read a book that changed my life: the newly released *The Wonderful, Spirit-Filled Life* by Charles Stanley. He shares his personal pilgrimage of learning to abide in the Holy Spirit. After a great struggle of frustration and fruitlessness, the Lord brought him face-to-face with the reality that we are not made to be fruit-producers, but fruit-bearers.

Stanley writes, "Jesus makes a clear delineation between the vine and the branch. The two are not the same. He is the vine; we are the branches. The two are joined, but are not one. The common denominator in nature is the sap. The sap is the life of the vine and its branches. Cut off the flow of the sap to the branch, and it slowly withers and dies."[xxi]

As a person learns to be filled with the Holy Spirit and walk in Him, the power Source inside of him produces godly character and maximizes his influence for Christ. Remember, it is not called *the fruit of you* but *the fruit of the Spirit.*

We are the vessel. He is the fountainhead.

Proving to Be His Disciples

Jesus said in John 15:8 that it brings the Father glory when we show we really are His disciples. Jesus Christ issued a simple call. He walked up to ordinary fishermen and said, *"Follow Me, and I will make you fishers of men"* (Matthew 4:19b, KJV). In other words, I will show you how to fish for people. The Message says, *"Come with me. I'll make a new kind of fisherman out of you. I'll show you how to catch men and women instead of perch and bass."* Then it says, *"They didn't ask questions, but simply dropped their nets and followed"* (Matthew 4:19-20, The Message).

Are you asking questions, or are you dropping your nets and following? Our mandate is none other than this first, clear call of the Lord: *follow Me and I will help you influence others for My kingdom.*

When Jesus left this earth, He gave us the Great Commission in Matthew 28:18-20. That mandate to make disciples involves going, baptizing, and teaching them to obey all things that Jesus taught. How will we teach others all the things Jesus taught? Through the process of discipleship or disciple-making.

Discipleship is simply the term we use to describe the process of teaching a new Christian how to follow Jesus and become a fisher of men. Robert Coleman writes, "The Great

Commission is not a special calling or gift of the Spirit; it is a command—an obligation incumbent upon the whole community of faith. There are no exceptions."[xxii]

In Matthew 28:18-20, as Jesus ended His earthly ministry, He basically told us, "Continue in the simple call of Jesus."

A shoe factory has one purpose: to produce shoes. Regardless of the manpower, effort, and money spent, if the factory does not produce shoes, it misses the mark. Likewise, a church can be active in a variety of endeavors and still not produce disciples. Churches have methodologies as wide as Jonah's whale. Yet we must use Jesus' methodology, which was men and women—leading them to salvation, making them disciples, and teaching them how to influence others. Our ministry is people, spreading God's amazing love to them with the intention of making them fully devoted followers of Christ.

Many churches have converts, those born again into the kingdom of God. But Jesus said to make disciples. The word disciple means "learner" or "follower." Learning involves knowing. Following involves obeying.

Jesus described this in John 14:21: *"Those who accept my commandments and obey them are the ones who love me. And because they love me, my Father will love them. And I will love them and reveal myself to each of them"* (NLT). That verse describes the life of a disciple. He loves Jesus. Because he loves Him, he obeys Him (as a follower). And as he obeys Jesus, the Lord makes Himself known to the disciple (as a learner). So, as you obey Jesus you come to know Him better.

As parents, when God entrusts a child to our care, our long-term goal is for them to grow up to become a fruit-bearing disciple of Jesus Christ, who fulfills his purpose in his generation and brings glory to the Lord.

Questions to Consider

1. How does knowing your children were created by God in His image affect your view of parenting?
2. What is the difference between bearing fruit and producing fruit?
3. What is the end goal for a Christian parent?

Prayer for this Week

Elohim, thank You for creating us for Your glory. In a world that pulls me in many directions, enable me to keep my focus on You and bearing fruit for Your name. May I grow as a disciple of Christ, and may we raise Christ-followers through our family.

If you want to skip to week two of Plans, head to page 105.

Week Three: Marks of a Disciple

A growing disciple is characterized by four consistent qualities:

- Abiding in God's Word (John 8:31-32)
- Obedience (Matthew 7:21; John 14:21)
- Spirit-controlled living (Ephesians 5:18; Galatians 5:16; Acts 6:5)
- Fruit-bearing (John 15:8,16)

Abiding in the Word of God

Jesus said, *"If you abide in my Word, you are truly my disciples"* (John 8:31b, ESV). A convert has not learned to abide, to live a lifestyle soaked in the Word of God. The psalmist describes the person who meditates on God's Word day and night (Psalm 1). God told Joshua the key to his success was meditating on the Book of the Law day and night (Joshua 1:8 NIV).

A disciple learns to feed himself. He doesn't depend on other people, his preacher, or his teachers. He gleans from these sources but knows how to go to the true Source. He is a person of the Book. As a growing disciple, he learns to grip God's Word by reading, hearing, meditating on, memorizing, and studying the Bible.

Obedience

A disciple of Communism obeys the teachings of Communism. A disciple of an outstanding voice instructor follows the instructions of that person. A disciple of an ice-skating coach follows the directions of that individual. So, a disciple of Jesus obeys Him.

How beautifully the fishermen illustrated this characteristic for us in Matthew 4 when they immediately dropped their nets. Peter practiced obedience again in Luke 5 when Jesus challenged him to throw the nets on the other side of the boat. The Bible records, *"'Master,' Simon replied, 'we worked hard all last night and didn't catch a thing. But if you say so, I'll let the nets down again'"* (vs. 5, NLT).

Here's a good litmus test for our discipleship: when Jesus speaks, do we obey? When you know what the Lord wants you to do, is your obedience immediate, or do you ask a lot of questions? If we don't obey God, it is because we don't love and trust Him.

Several years ago, I toured the InTouch Ministries facilities in Atlanta, Georgia, the home of the worldwide teaching ministry of Dr. Charles Stanley. Inscribed in large, bold letters on the lobby's wall is his well-known phrase, *Obey God and leave all of the consequences to Him.* Stanley says, "You do what the Lord tells you to do regardless of the circumstances or dangers you face, and you trust Him to make a path for you where there appears to be no way through."[xxiii]

Spirit-Controlled Living

When the disciples walked with Jesus, they literally *walked* with Him. They woke up in the morning, looked at Jesus, and thought, "Today, I'm with Him." In our day, in the Church Age, God left us the Holy Spirit. He comes alongside us to help, comfort, convict, guide, and most importantly, manifest the Person and Presence of Jesus.

Only Christians filled with and controlled by the Holy Spirit can please God and carry out His will. The fleshly, natural, carnal Christian cannot please God. At salvation we get all of the Spirit of God. The appropriate question then for the believer is not "Do you have the Spirit?" but "Does the Spirit have you?"

Missionaries Martha Franks and Bertha Smith participated in the great Shantung Revival in China of 1930, what some historians call the greatest revival and spiritual awakening of Baptist church history. During that move of God, many believers realized they were not filled with the Spirit of God. Selfishness ruled their lives, and God's Spirit could not flow from their innermost beings (John 7:37-39). The Spirit pours out when Jesus is on the throne. Bertha Smith wrote: "Since the work of the Holy Spirit is to magnify Christ, we are then, by an act of faith, to appropriate the Holy Spirit to come out of that crowded corner and fill us. He will fill up all of the space formerly occupied by self."[xxiv]

Are you filled by the Spirit of God? Are you walking under His direction and in submission to His leading? There can be no fulness of the Spirit without a life of yielding and moment-by-moment dependence.

Fruit-Bearing

In the Old Testament, the Lord filled His house with glory, which evoked tremendous awe and worship. After God removed His presence from the Old Testament Temple, the glory did not return until Jesus Christ came to earth. Just before He went back to the Father, Jesus explained that today the temple of the Lord is filled with glory through the process of fruit-bearing. Fruit-bearing disciples bring the Father glory.

We can bear the fruit of godly character. As the Spirit controls us, He produces the fruit of the Spirit (Galatians 5:22-23) and the fruit of righteous living. So, when you bear patience, joy, love, and gentleness and when you obey God, the temple is filled with glory. As you share Christ's work with others, He empowers you to be His witness, leading others to Christ and helping them be His disciples. And God is glorified. Is that not the simple call of Jesus?

Making Disciples of Our Children

Raising children to be fruit-bearing disciples may be the most overlooked method of accomplishing the Great Commission in our churches. For more than forty years, I've heard churches emphasize neighborhood outreach programs, mission trips, discipleship studies, and missionary support as a means to win people to Christ and make disciples. All of those good outlets have their place, but the Christian family remains the most powerful tool for producing disciples.

With the birth of a baby, God entrusts a couple with about eighteen years to invest deeply into that life. Wise parents begin with the end in mind. We want our son or daughter to grow into a life-long follower of Christ who influences others for Jesus and impacts the world.

I began praying for my future children when I was a freshman in college. I remember lying on my dormitory bed on the third floor of Bailey Dorm at Presbyterian College in South Carolina, asking God to bless their future lives, bring them to Christ, and fulfill His purposes for them. My wife's discovery that she was pregnant with our first child joyfully overwhelmed me with the reality of my fast-approaching fatherhood. Part of my preparation for fatherhood during Tracey's pregnancy in 2000 was two-fold.

First, I read James Dobson's excellent book *Straight Talk to Men: Timeless Principles for Leading Your Family.* Dobson challenges men to step up to the plate and be godly servant-leaders for their families. Second, I chose to go on a forty-day fast. I believed fasting and praying was one way to draw near to God for His blessing and power, and I knew I needed those in order to be a godly husband and dad. For eight weeks, I fasted from breakfast Monday to Friday and spent that time praying. For some of you, skipping breakfast is no big deal. But to me, especially when I was twenty-seven, missing a meal involved sacrifice. A funny thing happened during that fast. The first couple of weeks I loaded up on sweet fruit drinks instead of eating breakfast, and I actually gained weight. Finally, I realized I needed to lay off the cran-grape and just drink water.

The prophet Malachi reminds us one of the purposes of a marriage covenant is to produce godly children: *"Didn't the Lord make you one with your wife? In body and spirit you are his. And what does he want? Godly children from your union"* (Malachi 2:15a, NLT). And later in the same book, the prophet ends the Old Testament by talking about the spirit of a prophet: *"His preaching will turn the hearts of fathers to their children, and the hearts of children to their fathers. Otherwise I will come and strike the land with a curse"* (4:6, NLT).

In this little Old Testament book, God reveals two realities about parents and children. God wants us to produce godly children. It should be normative for Jesus-loving dads and moms to raise children who grow into Jesus-loving adults. We can have a vision to raise doctors, lawyers, judges, screenplay writers, architects, and teachers who love Him and want to bear His fruit and impact their cultures. And secondly, Malachi says one of the greatest achievements of the gospel going forth happens when the hearts of fathers and children turn toward each other. When parents and children love each other.

I love Bob Briner's challenge in his book *Roaring Lambs: A Gentle Plan to Radically Change Your World:* "I've always wondered why we could be so quick to sacrifice our children to become missionaries but stand in the way of their becoming broadcast journalists, film and television actors, photographers, and painters. ... If we are to be obedient to our Lord's call to go into all the world, we will begin reentering the fields that we have fled."[xxv]

When Hendrix began college a few years ago, I remembered that forty-day fast years ago. And I thank God that today my son is a fine Christian young man who takes the Lord seriously. He and I enjoy a relationship marked by mutual admiration and respect. The Lord answered all of those prayers, helping us raise a son who loves God and loves his family.

On Tuesdays, I pray for our family to embrace God's purposes in this world.

Questions to Consider

1. Is your life consistently characterized by obedience to the Lord?
2. Do you seek daily to live under the fulness of God's Spirit?
3. How can your family prioritize raising Jesus-followers?

Prayer for this Week

Father, the world sends so many mixed messages about the values we should embrace. Empower me to consistently work with You at the task of raising children who become godly adults who love You and want to bear Your fruit and impact their cultures.

If you want to skip to week three of Plans, head to page 113.

Week Four: Maximizing Your Influence

Parents and grandparents can take seriously the call to raise our children. Here are three reminders for that task:

- Maximize the family table.
- Value time at home.
- Be a filter.

Maximize the Family Table

Mealtimes offer rich opportunities for influencing the next generation. Practice listening to your children. Ask lots of questions. I know, when they become teens, they won't want to always answer. That's okay. Ask anyway. Create a family culture of knowing what's going on in each other's lives.

Then, practice sharing—from your own life and from God's Word. Include them in your inner story. Tell them about your day. Share thoughts, feelings, and desires.

The family table presents a captive audience for you to share from the Bible. Doing so creates an atmosphere of respect for God's Word. Sometimes after supper I say, "Okay, everybody clean your plates and come back with a Bible." We spend a few minutes together looking at a verse or passage.

Value Time at Home

Speed and overcommitment are curses of our age. In *Raising Kids in a Safe Home,* Josh and Christi Straub write: "An anti-Sabbath culture is an anti-family culture. For the sake of modeling a healthy lifestyle for our kids, we must learn to slow down and implement a regular day of rest into our family."[xxvi]

Guard against the cultural norm to keep your kids overloaded with activities outside of the home, particularly when they are young. The long-term value of unhurried time at home with a stable, happy family far outweighs the benefit of being at soccer every Monday, art every Tuesday, and kung fu every Thursday. We try to allow each child to be involved in one extra-curricular activity every semester.

Staying at home goes for parents too. Wayne Cordiero advises pastors to guard their schedules to be home regularly four nights a week. As a parent, I never regretted one evening I stayed home and put my children to bed. On two of those routine occasions, I had the opportunity to lead two of my children to Christ. We knelt in their bedrooms as they invited the Lord into their young lives.

When my children were babies, I made the decision to stay at home with my family on Saturdays. Instead of hanging out with my buddies playing tennis, bowling, or golfing, I knew my wife and children deserved my presence. Through the years, we all looked forward to Saturdays as a family day.

One year, when my children were preschoolers, my wife and kids headed off to the beach for a week with her parents while I stayed home and worked. When they left, the house suddenly became quiet, and I sat at our kitchen table and penned the following poem:

A Clean House One Day

There is coming a day when our house will be straight,
No Legos on the den floor, no beach towels on the gate.

I won't trip over Star Wars men in the middle of the night,
And he won't ask me when I come home
if we can wrestle and fight.

The train table and its many parts will
have long been stored away,
And we will have a clean floor and tidy
house instead on that day.

The yard will no longer overflow with
balls, bikes, and swings,
And I won't find in every nook, cranny, and
room baby dolls, stickers, and rings.

Crayons will not be found, spills less frequent, and diapers no more,
Except for a few crayon marks penned
long ago on a wall, table, or floor.

Yes, Mom and Dad, there is coming a day
when your house will not be cluttered,
For the day will arrive when your child moves
away, and then your heart will flutter.

And you will recall olden days of toys, games, and snacks.
The dress-up clothes will be gone, no cow-
boy hats on the racks.

Dad, forget the golf course. Your hobbies can
wait for these oh so precious years.
Stay at home, be silly and play, and give a listening ear.

Mom, make your family number one after faith in God.
Care for them and share your love, like
a shepherd's firm but gentle rod.

So please be patient in these years to remember what really matters.
Enjoy your children, embrace them now, and
thank God for spilled-milk splatters!

Remember, influence occurs through relationships. And lasting relationships take intentional time spent together.

Be a Filter

"The art of leadership is not saying yes; it is saying no," said former British Prime Minister Tony Blair.[xxvii] One of life's great challenges is learning to not just go with the flow because sometimes the flow goes in the wrong direction. We live in a day of great distraction. Because of the digital age, information flows constantly. Some say we have become the society that is looking down, always checking our phones, tablets, and devices. These weapons of mass distraction cause us at times to miss some important things in life.

Our children need help filtering the world's messages. A day existed in our country when children received the same basic worldview at home, church, school, and in entertainment. Today, the messages they receive at school and from culture often conflict with Christianity. Children hear ideas from public education and modern entertainment that include the secular or godless, views of evolution, same-sex marriage, gender confusion, and moral relativism. Parents, we must be vigilant in teaching our kids how to filter these messages through the Word of God.

We teach our children how to think as we discuss thoughts, ideas, and movements in history and culture. We use resources written and produced by evangelicals to help shape their minds. We introduce them to believers who share a biblical view of life. And we keep the long-term goal in mind. We are reproducing godly offspring, fruit-bearing disciples of Jesus Christ.

I've heard the average home in America keeps the television on seven hours a day with the average viewer watching between twenty and thirty-six hours a week. Many families can't sit through a meal without everyone checking their phones. Some couples take their tablets to bed, unable to endure the detachment.

Jesus came to give us abundant life in the real world—not a virtual one. As parents, we all know how easy it is to give in to electronic systems. Instead of quality time, we opt for the babysitting of the television. Instead of encouraging intellectual or spiritual stimulation, we choose the instant gratification of the internet. How can we parents create space in our families to raise fruit-bearing disciples of Jesus Christ? Here are several suggestions for ways to say no to the constant lure of the digital world.

Play games together.

Make a collection of board games. Develop the habit of occasionally clearing the table for game night. As children get older, families can invest in games that take longer to play. Some that our family enjoys are A Ticket to Ride, Shadows over Camelot, and, of course, Monopoly. Playing board games allows for lots of interaction and often leads to laughter.

Talk and listen.

It amazes me to see families sit down in restaurants, take out all their devices, and never talk to each other until the food comes. Make family mealtime a time of conversation. Declare meals a no-electronics zone. Linger at the table as much as possible. Ask questions of your children. And listen. I heard Henry Blackaby once say that because he wanted to have a meaningful relationship with his children when they became adults, he knew that meant he needed to have lots of conversations about superheroes when they were young children. Listen to what they share from their lives.

Set boundaries.

Dr. Archibald Hart and his daughter, Sylvia, wrote a helpful book called *The Digital Invasion: How Technology is Shaping You and Your Relationships.* In it they explore the clinical effects of the digital age and offer solutions to guard your mind, body, and spirit. Digital technology has become controlling, addictive, and intrusive. The Harts write, "Digital technology has a good side. It also has a dark side. Increasing digital overuse is already harming parts of our physical, emotional, relational, and spiritual health." Parents, it's okay for you to be the bad guy about the use of electronics. Don't let culture squeeze you into its form. It has always been the responsibility of a parent to monitor their children and keep them away from unhealthy distractions. Our children don't need endless hours of internet and television exposure. Scientific studies show that too much digital time actually alters our brain patterns.[xxviii] For our family, screen time isn't allowed during the week unless all school work is complete. On the weekends, our children may have up to two hours of screen time a day.

Go outside.

God created us to interact with His natural world. Lead your children to enjoy the outdoors and engage in physical exercise outside the walls of your house. Children still need time to play in the dirt, walk in the woods, and expand their own imaginations.

G. K. Chesterton said, "Don't ever take a fence down until you learn the reason it was put up."[xxix] We live in a day where society tells us to live without fences or boundaries. Friends, remember, if "everything goes," then nothing remains. Our children need fences to help them navigate this crazy world.

On Tuesdays, I pray that my family walks in God's purposes. Our Shepherd leads us in the specific paths He has for each of us.

Questions to Consider

1. How can you practically maximize your family table, making it a place for connection and discipleship?
2. What can you do to guard and value family time at home?
3. Look for ways to be a filter for the messages your children receive from the world.

Prayer for this Week

Father, embracing Your values runs counter to so much of the world's rat race. Give me wisdom and courage to set appropriate boundaries for my family. Help us to keep a long-term perspective and realize how fleeting the days are when our children and grandchildren are young.

If you want to skip to week four of Plans, head to page 121.

PRAYER POINTS FOR PURPOSES

1. Pray they will grow as fruit-bearing disciples of Jesus Christ:
   - Abiding in the Word of God.
   - Obeying consistently.
   - Allowing the Spirit of God to control.
   - Bearing fruit in godly character, the fruit of the Spirit, and influence on others.

2. Ask God to enable you as parents to be disciple-makers of your children and grandchildren:
   - Maximize the time spent at the family table.
   - Value your time together and at home.
   - Be a filter for your children.

3. Pray for each family member to grow in maturity—mentally, spiritually, physically, and emotionally.
   - That they will learn to read well, think, and stretch their minds around great ideas.
   - For them to grow in love for and intimacy with the Lord.
   - For them to honor God with the way they take care of and use their bodies.
   - That they will have emotional strength, not tossed around whimsically and without substance.

4. Ask the Lord to work in your family's culture so that you honor Him and love each other.
   - Growing in respect for each other.
   - Learning to bear with and put up with each other's weaknesses.
   - Choosing to serve one another.

Week One: God's Perspective

The Plans of God

Not only does God have general purposes for our lives, but He has specific plans for each person. Devin Brown, author of *Hobbit Lessons: A Map for Life's Unexpected Journeys,* writes:

> Adventures come in many forms, but they always mean something new for us. And what is new is always somewhat mysterious.[xxx]

Bilbo Baggins experienced this in *The Hobbit.* When he stepped out his front door after breakfast one day and met Gandalf the Wizard, "he had no idea that adventure was about to come knocking."[xxxi]

Similarly, when Gideon threshed wheat in that lonely wine-press beside the oak at Ophrah, he had no idea adventure was knocking on his door. But God had plans. And when Gideon discovered God as his peace, he was ready to embark on the journey of a lifetime.

The entire faith-life is one continuous experience of trusting God. And trusting God, shown through our obedience, allows God to maximize our influence. Gideon's account in Judges 6 and 7 shows us five realities about trusting God in His plans for us:

- God's presence is our strength in trials and tests (6:11-16).
- God will require us to challenge the system and status quo (6:28-35).
- God will prove Himself to us to answer our fears and doubts (6:36-40).
- God can move heaven and earth to send us encouragement (7:9-15).
- God sometimes requires us to do that which seems unreasonable (7:16-22).

God's Presence is Our Strength in Trials and Tests

Gideon may have thought the angel crazy when he called him a mighty hero. But God's presence can change everything.

Henry Blackaby's workbook *Experiencing God: Knowing and Doing the Will of God* significantly impacted my life. He writes:

> God is an extremely realistic God. He was in Scripture. He is the same today. When He provided manna, quail, and water for the children of Israel, He was being helpful. When Jesus fed five thousand people, He was being practical. The God I see revealed in Scripture is real, personal, and practical.[xxxii]

The presence of God is the one reality that marks the people of God as belonging to Him. Many religions, civic groups, and schools have moral codes. But only God's people have His presence. As He leads His people, sometimes He takes us into confusing circumstances involving loss, defeat, and confusion. One of the precious promises from the Bible is that God will never leave us.

Occasionally, what we see with our eyes is the opposite of what we hear from the Lord. Three times the Scripture says in Judges that Gideon's circumstances didn't confirm what God said. They actually reflected the opposite. And every time the Lord answered by simply promising His presence.

First, circumstances find Gideon threshing wheat in the winepress, hiding and alone. Yet the angel says, *"Mighty hero, the Lord is with you!"* (6:12, NLT).

Then Gideon asks the why question: *"Sir, if the Lord is with us, why has all this happened to us?"* (6:13, NLT). The Lord answers by saying, *"Go with the strength you have, and rescue Israel from the Midianites. I am sending you!"* (6:14, NLT).

Third, Gideon asks the *how* question: *"How can I rescue Israel? My clan is the weakest ... and I am the least in my entire family!"* (6:15, NLT). The angel's response: *"I will be with you"* (6:16, NLT).

Do you see the progression? Negative circumstances show one set of figures. But God keeps promising His presence.

Like Gideon, we like to question why and how. We see past failures, regrets, or disappointments and wonder why. We look at present resources and opportunities and look toward the future, wondering how. *How could I ever get a good job when I lost one? How can I ever recover from losing a child or going through a divorce? How can I ever afford to educate my children?*

I was invited to preach at my home church in Greenville,

South Carolina, my senior year of college. Speaking to a church of about seven hundred people was no small task for a twenty-one-year-old. Charles Stanley says your home church is the worst place to ever preach, because people remember when you were a boy, and they think, "Oh, isn't that cute?"

Even though twenty-four years have passed since then, I still remember sitting on the platform listening to Dr. Earl Crumpler introduce me. As I waited, fear overcame me and I thought, *There is no possible way I can do this.* Instantly, I remembered the story of Gideon. It was as if the Holy Spirit said to me, *If you will get up and start speaking, I will be with you and help you.* As an act of faith, I chose to stand and begin preaching. A lady in the audience later told me, "I could tell when you started speaking and the Holy Spirit took over." Since then, I have preached, taught, and spoken to groups hundreds of times. I don't think I ever get up to speak that I don't mentally rehearse the exchange between Gideon and the angel. I boldly affirm in my spirit, *I can't, Lord, but you can.*

Your battle may not be preaching a sermon. It may be dealing with a bad-attitude teenager. Or facing a pile of debt. Or confronting a problem in your office or church. Or helping an aging loved one. Whatever it is, the challenge seems daunting, leaving you feeling small. God's promise to you is the same as to Gideon. He does not explain all the *whys* of yesterday. Nor does He tell you all the details of *how* for the future. But He does promise, "I will be with you."

So, take the next step and count on His presence.

God's Perspective

One of the hardest disciplines in the Christian life is learning to see life from God's perspective—to think God's thoughts instead of our own. If we only follow our limited reasoning, we may completely miss what God is doing. Think of these examples:

Example One: Isaiah wrote, *"'My thoughts are nothing like your thoughts,' says the Lord. 'And my ways are far beyond anything you could imagine. For just as the heavens are higher than the earth, so my ways are higher than your ways and my thoughts higher than your thoughts'"* (55:8-9, NLT).

Example Two: Jesus set up a situation to prove His greatness. He planned to feed five thousand men from only a boy's small lunch. Like a master teacher, He asked Philip where they would find bread to feed the crowd. John almost comically tells us, *"He asked this only to test him, for He already had in mind what He was going to do"* (John 6:6, NIV). Matthew's account tells us the disciples then told Jesus, *"Send the crowds away"* (14:15, NIV). In other words, the disciples had a meeting without Jesus, and their best long-range, strategic planning said to send the crowds home. Maybe they patted each other on the back for their frugal common sense. However, their long-range planning did not include Jesus. And His thoughts were different than theirs.

Example Three: When Jesus told the disciples He had to die, His buddy Peter rebuked Him. Imagine rebuking Jesus. He said that he would *never* let Jesus die. Notice the Lord's response. It is one of the most chilling ones in Scripture: *"Jesus turned to Peter and said, 'Get away from me, Satan! You are a dangerous trap to me. You are seeing things merely from a human point of view, not from God's'"* (Matthew 16:23, NLT).

Yikes! These and other scriptural examples show that even the people closest to Jesus can completely miss Him. Left to our own planning, we may become a "dangerous trap" to Jesus. The Lord was saying to Gideon that He was "much more concerned with what you are going to become than with what you are. Gideon, I don't see you for what you are now, but for what you are going to be, because I am with you." Though people see our failures and rough edges, God views us through the power of our divine potential.[xxxiii]

Next week we'll continue looking at what it means to walk in God's plans.

Questions to Consider

1. How, like Bilbo, have you experienced adventures appearing in your life when you least expected them?
2. In what part of your life currently do you most need the reminder that even in trials and tests, God is with you?
3. Why is it so easy for us to think so much smaller than the Lord?

Prayer for this Week

Father, it is so difficult for me to look at life through Your perspective and not lean on my own understanding. Open my eyes daily to see You more, think more like You, and impart Your thoughts to my family.

If you want to skip to week one of Purity, head to page 127.

Week Two: Trusting God through Change

God Will Require Us to Challenge the System and Status Quo

Gideon's first test occurred in his daddy's front yard. Joash shows how far Israel sank, allowing the Canaanite religions to mix with their own. In his yard stood the town's altar to Baal and an Asherah pole. If you don't know, Baal was a Canaanite false god, and Asherah was his girlfriend. Baal and Asherah worship included immorality and wicked, pagan sacrifices. Evidently, the townspeople tried to appease both Jehovah and Baal.

As the angel moved Gideon toward God's plans, he instructed him to tear down the altar in Joash's yard. In other words, God couldn't do a great work through Gideon until he dealt with the sin at his own house. The idols of others must be broken before he could set up God's altar. False gods must fall before the true One reigns.

As we pray for God to work in our families, He may start revealing our sins. He may tell us to first deal with our own problems. Get some help with our habitual anger. Make a budget and stay on it. Forgive our parents and choose to love them. Stop playing around with internet porn and get some accountability.

He may require us to confront something in the life of someone around us. Maybe as we pray for our children or grandchildren, we see a bad habit forming in their lives. Or we realize they are developing friendships with bad influences. Perhaps they latch on to false ideas.

In the United States of America, our idols are not made of wood and stone. Today, our idols are primarily idols of the mind. We live in a culture that has largely rejected the Word of God—God's thoughts. We are living in the days of judgment described in Romans 1, when *"they began to think up foolish ideas of what God was like. As a result, their minds became dark and confused. Claiming to be wise, they instead became utter fools"* (21b-22, NLT).

Because of the availability of the internet, both true and false ideas are shared constantly. The main idols of our culture include false ideas contrary to what God says. One of the enormous lies of our day with immeasurable consequences came from Charles Darwin's *On the Origin of Species*. His theory, completely devoid of God, gave way to naturalism in the modern world. Naturalism sees man as the center of the universe.

Though Darwin majored in theology, he grew angry and bitter toward God. After the death of his young daughter and son, he raged in his heart. Later, his writings spurred on a theory of existence which completely removes a Creator as well as any absolute truth, personal accountability, or universal moral laws. "As he worked as an amateur naturalist, he seethed in his heart toward a God who would cause such misery and suffering as he was experiencing. And instead of trusting—he continued to wallow in the scum of indicting God."[xxxiv]

Genesis 1:1 provides the initial building block of our entire faith system. Everything started with Elohim, the personally involved Creator. He is the Source. He knows us by name. Every major Christian doctrine finds its root in Genesis 1-11. How crafty of the serpent, the great deceiver, to spin and spread a lie from a bitter man's writings to cast doubt on the beginnings of the Bible. Today we need a gospel understanding that begins with Genesis 1:1.

Without the Creator, Elohim, there is ultimately no foundation for morality or ethics. Once you embrace a worldview without intelligent design, you abandon the concept of God, ultimate purpose, and morality's basis. My family recently watched Ben Stein's documentary *Expelled: No Intelligence Allowed.* He interviews numerous scientists around the world, showing how educators and scientists are ridiculed, denied tenure, and even fired for believing nature gives evidence of Intelligent Design. The documentary explains how Darwinism is the strongest engine in academia fueling atheism.

If your son or daughter goes to a public school or university, he or she will be educated in this false idea. During my oldest son's senior year of high school, he took one class at the local state university. What a shock that for European Civilizations the teacher spent the first two days defending the theory of evolution as essential to understanding the history of Europe. What does that have to do with European Civilizations? Well, it has to do with framework and worldview. Naturalism and secularism need the foundation of the theory of evolution—a world void of God and thus void of accountability to Him.

Lawyer and author Dennis Prager has warned for years that the secular Left—as opposed to classic conservatives or classic liberals—has taken over most of our public colleges and universities, turning them into indoctrination breeding grounds for the false ideas of naturalism.[xxxv]

Families and churches have not always done a great job of helping young people gain an intelligent understanding of our faith. Dr. Howard Hendricks said in 1980, the greatest sin of the American church is the failure to think. Parents and grandparents, you must be ready to deal with the idols of our society—false ideas that set themselves up against God and His Word![xxxvi]

God Will Prove Himself to Us to Answer Our Fears and Doubts

Gideon prayed to Elohim and asked for the second sign, wanting God to prove Himself in a certain way. Gideon put out a wool fleece on the threshing floor at night. In the morning he wanted the fleece wet but the ground dry. God obliged, but Gideon was not satisfied. He asked again, this time for the fleece to be dry and the ground wet. And the Bible says, *"During the night, Elohim did what Gideon asked. The wool was dry, but all the ground was covered with dew"* (Judges 6:40, NOG).

An old evangelist told me when I started in ministry and faced a decision, "You just need to throw out a fleece. That's the Bible way. Throw out a fleece and see what God does." Well, while I don't question his sincerity, I think that is bad biblical interpretation and application. The Bible does not tell us to throw out fleeces. What is evident in this and other biblical accounts is how gracious our God is to meet His people when we are afraid and confused.

The prophet Jeremiah wrote to troubled people: *"Then you will call on me and come and pray to me, and I will listen to you. You will seek me and find me when you seek me with all your heart"* (Jeremiah 29:12-13, NIV). When we want to follow the Lord but don't know what to do, when we question the road ahead, when we need reassurance, it is okay to honestly go to the Lord and say, "I need You. I need help. Please show Yourself to me."

One of my favorite Bible promises is 2 Chronicles 16:9a: *"For the eyes of the Lord range throughout the earth to strengthen those whose hearts are fully committed to him"* (NIV). When your heart is seeking the Lord, He has a million means at His disposal to show Himself to you. That doesn't mean you ask for a sign. It does mean you ask Him to show Himself. And that is better than a sign.

God Reminds Us of Our Weaknesses so We Rely on Him and Not Ourselves

The venerable missionary-statesman Hudson Taylor said, "All

God's giants have been weak men who did great things for God because they reckoned on God being with them."[xxxvii]

In an unusual and unexpected test, God reduces Gideon's army from ten thousand warriors to three hundred. In human terms, they would be outnumbered 450 to one. Herein lies an essential spiritual reality: God allows us to experience weakness so that we rely on Him.

The Lord does not want us trusting anything more than Himself. Not a plan, not a friend, not a bank account. He regularly works to teach us He is our source. Everything else He uses is simply a resource. And sometimes, He lets us go through great need in order to get our eyes on Him and prepare us for His provision.

On Wednesdays, I ask God to help us to walk in the plans He has for each of our lives, maximizing our God-given potential.

"It is a process that is repeated many times in the Word of God. When God wants a man or woman to do great things for Him, He builds into that man or woman not self-confidence but God-confidence." —Gary Inrig, *Hearts of Iron, Feet of Clay* [xxxviii]

Questions to Consider

1. What idols of ideas do you regularly encounter in the culture?
2. Why is it important to believe Genesis 1:1 and teach your children a worldview that embraces that reality?
3. Where do you need to ask God to answer your fears and doubts?

Prayer for this Week

Father, You promise Your people that if we seek You with all of our hearts, we will find You. Help me to not be half-hearted in my asking, seeking, and knocking. Thank You for being a greater treasure than anything this world offers.

If you want to skip to week two of Purity, head to page 135.

Week Three: Faith During the Impossible

God Can Move Heaven and Earth to Send Us Encouragement

When God was ready to give His boy victory, He knew Gideon still needed one extra oomph of encouragement. Gideon dealt with fear and doubt. He heard God and wanted to believe Him, but at every step he saw overwhelming obstacles. The Lord graciously continued to meet him and send help. Gideon felt inadequate for the overwhelming task and doubted if God was in this huge assignment.

Sometimes tasks from the Lord make sense to us. Other times they are so out of our comfort zone—and so beyond human capability—that we need extra confirmation from the Lord that He is indeed involved.

The word encourage literally means "to fill with courage." To be encouraged is to be lifted in spirit and confidence. "To encourage" means "to call beside." *The American Woman's Bible* says, "When we encourage, we are coming alongside someone else, cheering them on. We are offering comfort and motivation ... they know they are not alone."[xxxix]

One of my best friends, Jay, heard the story of Daniel Nash, a prayer warrior for the nineteenth-century preacher Charles Finney. Before Finney's crusades and revival meetings, Nash quietly slipped into town several weeks prior to the meetings and began praying. The godly man gave himself continually to pray on behalf of Finney, praying for the outpouring of the Holy Spirit on those meetings.

Jay and I attended the same church, and when I preached, Jay quietly slipped out of the sanctuary and retreated into a room that became his prayer room. While I preached, Jay prayed for God to work. Once, I preached a sermon challenging men to be godly heroes for their families. I vividly remember seeing Jay slip out when I began preaching. The Spirit of God moved that Sunday, and about thirty men came to the altar to pray in response to the message. Jay's faithfulness to pray as I preached was a great encouragement.

God is able to send encouragement. It may be through a verse of Scripture, a song on the radio, an email, or a divinely-orchestrated circumstance. In Gideon's case, God told him to go down into the Midianite camp with his servant. In the middle of the night, they slipped in unnoticed. With thousands of tents, God providentially guided them to a specific one, where a man just had a dream of Gideon and his men smashing the Midianite camp. The Bible says, *"When Gideon heard the dream and its interpretation, he bowed in worship before the Lord. Then he returned to the Israelite camp and shouted, 'Get up! For the Lord has given you victory over the Midianite hordes!'"* (Judges 7:15, NLT). That encounter was all Gideon needed to fill him with courage. God worked in the other camp on his behalf.

The summer following my senior year of college, the Promise Keepers (PK) movement swept the country. Men filled stadiums across the nation to hear exhortation and encouragement from God's Word. The summer of 1995, PK held a stadium event in Atlanta, Georgia, at the Philips Arena. I lived in Greenville, South Carolina, with my parents, 150 miles away. I wanted to attend PK, but could not afford a ticket. I told no one of my desire to go.

The week of the event, our church had a Vacation Bible School each evening. On Wednesday night, I kept thinking about PK but saw no way to make it happen. Besides, two days before the rally meant it was a sold-out event. Taking a break from VBS duties, I slipped into a dark classroom, sat, and voiced a prayer of faith. "Lord, I have no way to purchase a ticket for Promise Keepers. But if you want me to go, I ask You to move heaven and earth to get a ticket for me. Amen." I committed it to the Lord and went on with my duties.

A few hours later, when I entered my house, my mother said, "Rhett, a lady from church called. She said her brother was going to Promise Keepers this weekend but suddenly had a change of plans. They want to know if you would like his ticket for free?"

You can imagine my excitement. Through that experience, I learned when God wants to do something, He is able to move any person and any resource to accomplish His will. Yes, He can move heaven and earth to respond to the prayer of faith—even a small one.

God Sometimes Requires Us to Do That Which Seems Unreasonable

God will lead us to impossible tasks in order to show us His strength, provision, and control. Taking three hundred men without any weapons—armed only with torches, clay pots, and trumpets—to fight an army of 135,000 does not make any sense, humanly speaking. Nor does feeding five thousand men with only two fish and five loaves of bread. Talk about some Wonder Bread!

But as we follow the Lord and listen to His Spirit, His instructions sometimes seem unreasonable. Consider the following:

- Moses picked up a snake in the wilderness by the tail and it transformed into a staff.
- Peter paid his taxes by picking up a random fish in the lake.
- Abraham prepared to kill his only son. Because the Patriarch knew Isaac came through God's promise, he believed the Lord would provide a substitute.
- God made Zechariah and Elizabeth wait for decades to have children—until they were senior adults, way past child-bearing age.
- Jesus told Peter, after a whole night of useless fishing, to throw the nets one more time on the other side of the boat.

God's instructions will not always make sense to us. When

they don't, we can either make excuses, or we can submit and obey.

Bents in the Babies

As parents and grandparents, we have the incredible task of partnering together to help our children discover their unique bent. An oft-misunderstood proverb reads, *"Train up a child in the way he should go, and when he is old he will not depart from it"* (Proverbs 22:6, NKJV). Many well-meaning adults believe this means if we give them enough biblical truth at young ages, the children will embrace those things when they become adults. While that does happen at times, I don't think that's the point of this verse. And that approach can lead to a very legalistic, grace-less style of training.

Instead, the idea in this verse focuses on God's creative design. Pastor Charles Swindoll explains that this Hebrew passage carries the idea that each child comes with a predetermined pattern or bent. One of the wonders of parenting—and one of the affirmations of Intelligent Design—is how each child is so different. One challenge of healthy parenting is discovering each child's uniqueness and learning to train them, or raise them up, in a way where they can develop their personal bent and maximize their divine potential.[xl]

Dan Miller wisely shares, "Look at how God has uniquely gifted you in your skills, abilities, personality traits, and values, dreams, and passions. It is in these that we find the authentic path designed for us for a purpose-driven life."[xli] In helping you discover these wonderful bents, I highly recommend Dan

Miller's book *48 Days to the Work You Love,* as well as Richard Bolles's *What Color is Your Parachute?*

The North American evangelical church has not always done a great job of teaching the biblical concept of vocation. Instead, we have sometimes adopted a mindset that says, "All that really matters is evangelism and getting people to heaven." This has sometimes created the idea that if you really want to serve God, you must be a preacher, missionary, or in some other type of clergy-related role. A biblical understanding of work, however, is rooted in the fact that our Creator made us in His image and for His glory. As the master Creator, He made a fascinating world filled with people with all kinds of gifts, skills, and passions. As we learn to develop our bents and pursue the giftedness unique to us, we bring Him glory and fulfill His purposes for us. We get our English word vocation from the Latin *vocare,* "to call." The idea of vocation suggests something specific to you. Something God-given calls out to you.

In Genesis 1:28, we find what theologians call The Cultural Mandate. In the very first chapter of the Scripture, the Lord gives His people two primary tasks: multiplication and dominion. In other words, reproduce people who follow God with their lives, which is what Jesus told his followers to do when He left this earth, and create culture that honors God and helps humanity. Charles Colson and Nancy Pearcy wrote, "The only task of the church, many fundamentalists and evangelicals have believed, is to save as many lost souls as possible from a world literally going to hell. But this implicit denial of a Christian worldview is unbiblical and is the reason we have lost so much influence in the world." The first task God assigned His people in Genesis 1 and 2 is known as The Cultural Mandate—creating and building culture that honors God, reflects Him, and helps people. Unfortunately, for decades the church in America often ignored that call.

Michael Novak adds that humans are "called to be co-creators with God, bringing forth the potentialities the Creator has hidden. Creation is full of secrets waiting to be discovered, riddles which human intelligence is expected by the Creator to unlock."[xlii]

So, with this incredible understanding, the lawyer, landscaper, mechanic, homeschool mom, hairdresser, artist, computer programmer, or life coach can bring glory to God and fulfill his calling just as much as the evangelist or missionary.

As we learn to embrace the creative design in our own lives and the lives of our children, the Bible says that God will place *"a new song in my mouth, a song of praise to our Elohim"* (Psalm 40:3, NAG). When Gideon chose to trust Elohim for His purposes and plans, God gave him a song worth singing. As we pray for our families, we can pray with confidence that Elohim has purposes and plans for our lives, our children's lives, and our grandchildren's.

Questions to Consider

1. When has the Lord given you encouragement when you needed it?

2. How has God challenged you in the past or the present to do something that seemed unreasonable by your natural senses?

3. What skills, abilities, personality traits, and dreams do you see in your children? How can you nurture those things for their futures?

Prayer for this Week

Father, thank You for the myriad of vocations—callings—for individuals to glorify You, serve other people, and meet needs in various seasons of their lives. Help me to prepare and train my children and grandchildren for the various ways You will call to them.

If you want to skip to week three of Purity, head to page 143.

Week Four: Riding the River

My family enjoys a lot of water activities, including tubing and kayaking. We've made numerous trips down Deep Creek in Bryson City, North Carolina, and the French Broad River in Brevard County. An exhilarating part of the journey is not being in control but simply going where the river takes you. Through calm patches, white water, and fast shoots, you learn to enjoy the journey as it comes.

Tonya Anthony Crawford is one of my oldest friends. We grew up together in church in Greenville, South Carolina, as children and teenagers. She recently shared with me about a part of the journey she and her husband Brian experienced when they were unsure of which path to take.

Expecting their first child years ago, they both worked full-time. Occasionally, she broached the subject with Brian of her resigning and staying at home. They would look over their financial spreadsheet and see that after they paid their monthly bills, little remained. It simply did not seem possible. Tonya would cry and they would pray together, but the numbers seemed black and white.

After their son's birth, Tonya endured a deep depression. She says, "Someone else held my son more than me. Brian saw it too—someone else was raising our child."

Tonya desperately began job-hunting, finally landing a part-time one with a non-profit. She put in her notice, thrilled for the opportunity. However, the day before starting the new job, they called and said the position was no longer available due to a decrease in grant funding. Tonya shared, "I was, a little by default, but primarily by God's gracious hand, officially a stay-at-home mom. Soon after, Brian received an unexpected promotion, which made up enough difference to maintain their bills. She says:

> I'll never forget Brian sitting at the computer putting in all the numbers for the month. We shouldn't have made it this week, but somehow we had money in the bank and under the mattress. To this day, we reflect on our sense of wonder how God provided for our little family."

It wouldn't be the last time either.

The year 2008 brought a significant recession to much of America. For the Crawfords, the impact required them to sell most of their material possessions. During 2009 and 2010, they seemed to live day and night on thin financial ice. One wrong move, and the ice would break.

For thirteen months, the Crawfords did not receive one paycheck, living off of their sold assets and Tonya's part-time babysitting job.

During the same time, their children were in first and second grade at a local school.

In spite of good teachers, the parents gradually became convicted they needed to begin homeschooling:

> My son's second grade homework took an absurd two hours each night. We spent hours in the car driving to school, ballet or sports practice, and church. We essentially slept, ate, and did homework at home and then lived Monday through Fridays in the car. We were miserable. It was during our worst financial years that God put homeschooling on our hearts, something I said I'd "never" do.

They began earnestly praying for direction. Tonya remembers saying to the Lord, "Really? You are putting this on my heart now? We are all but destitute. I don't want to homeschool." But she began reading, talking to people, researching, and making a list of pros and cons. None of their friends supported it—not a single one. They scoffed, justifying their reasons for putting their kids in a corporate school environment and why it was important. Their parents were silent on the issue, which they later came to appreciate.

Finally, they knew the Lord was showing them to begin homeschooling: "With each passing day, and hours upon hours of prayer, the conviction became like a vice grip on our hearts. Without any financial security and only one friend in the homeschool community at the time to give us guidance and encouragement, we set out on a new path."

Today, those children are well-rounded, independent, strong, and self-sufficient. Two of them are currently in college at Clemson University. Tonya shares:

> Twenty-five years of marriage and adulthood has taught us that it's okay to be afraid or uncertain, but we benefit great-

ly from trusting His hand in our lives. When fear threatens my spirit, all I have to do is recount His guiding hand in our lives, trust His loving and all-powerful hand, and be obedient to His calling.

We never know which way the river runs. But when the calm water suddenly turns into churning white water, we learn to trust that our Shepherd is ahead of us, knows the way, and will lead us along the journey. As we seek to shepherd our own families, may we rest in the knowledge of Him.

Questions to Consider

1. What emotions do you think Brian and Tonya went through as they walked on thin financial ice?
2. Where in your life may the Lord be drying up one plan in order to direct you to a new one?
3. Just as God directed the Crawfords in His plans, He can and will direct you and your family. How can you worry less and trust more as you ride life's river?

Prayer for this Week

Father, I'm tempted to worry and fret when my plans don't go as expected. Help me to remember Your faithfulness. When life's river becomes white with rapids, keep my focus on You and help me to trust instead of fret.

If you want to skip to week four of Purity, head to page 149.

PRAYER POINTS FOR PLANS

Elohim created your family and wants to guide them into His purposes and plans. Here are five ways to pray for the Creator to make us the kind of people He wants us to be:

1. Pray they will know and obey the will of God for their lives (Colossians 1:9).
   - Filled with the knowledge of His will through spiritual wisdom and understanding.
   - Living a life worthy of the Lord to please Him.
   - Strengthened with His power to have great endurance, patience, and joy.
   - Giving thanks to the Father.

2. Pray they will, like King David, fulfill their purpose in their generation (Acts 13:36).
   - Remembering that God does have plans for them (Jeremiah 29:11).
   - Asking that they may thrive in the various seasons of their lives (Ecclesiastes 3:1).
   - Asking for His purposes and plans to be fulfilled in and through them (Proverbs 16:4; 19:21).

3. Ask the Lord to enable them to trust Him as they walk in His plans.
   - May they be strengthened by God's presence.
   - May they reject false ideas from the world, replacing them with truth.
   - May they learn to depend on God in their weaknesses.

- May they learn to find strength and encouragement in the Lord.

4. Ask that each family member grow to maximize their God-given potential:
   - Discover their God-given bents.
   - Mature in their unique skills, abilities, personality traits, and passions.
   - Find work that is fulfilling, meaningful, and profitable.
   - Learn to carefully take risks and never stop growing and learning.

5. Pray for current and future generations of your family:
   - To come to know the Lord personally.
   - To fear, love, obey, and serve Him.
   - To continue passing on a godly legacy.

Week One: Discipline in Purity

Like most teenagers, I enjoyed making my friends laugh. Most of my teen years took place in the great decade of the 1980s. We sang to Whitney, Chicago, and Alabama, watched *Steel Magnolias, Back to the Future,* and *Batman,* and met on Saturday evenings at Taco Bell to enjoy their ninety-nine-cent menu. One bad habit young people often adopt—particularly boys—is the habit of putting each other down in order to put self on top. Sometimes a teen will say or do anything for a good laugh from his peer group.

Though I generally walked the line, I adopted bad habits of saying things around my friends I would never dare repeat to my parents. An occasional profanity, a sexually crude comment, or simply making fun of someone to please the guys would come out. At the same time, I was heavily involved in our church's youth group. We had an outstanding youth pastor and a great group of adult volunteers who loved us and wanted to help us learn to follow Jesus. Our youth ministry offered many opportunities to be exposed to God's Word and motivated us to live for Him.

During my junior year of high school, I read Ephesians 4:29 for the first time: *"Do not let any unwholesome talk come out of your mouths, but only what is helpful for building others up according to their needs, that it may benefit those who listen"* (NIV). I don't remember where I was when I first saw those words, but the Holy Spirit began His penetrating work of conviction. I knew my practice was a far cry from Paul's exhortation. Our church trained us to memorize Scripture, so I decided to hide that one in my heart, which I did. To this day, more than thirty years later, I can still quote that one word for word.

Without my knowing it, God enrolled me into His school of holiness. Now lest you think you graduate from that one, as I write, I have just begun my fiftieth year, and school is still in session.

Taming the Tongue

One passage to consider is Psalm 119:9 and 11: *"How can a young man keep his way pure? By keeping it according to Your Word. I have treasured Your Word in my heart, so that I may not sin against You"* (NASB). This chapter, the Mount Everest of the Psalter, praises the Word of God as one of our greatest helps toward holiness. The psalmist promises that the regular intake, meditation on, and application of Scripture helps a young person avoid sin and walk with the Lord.

Today, I probably rate Ephesians 4:29 and that lesson of controlling my speech as one of the greatest lessons of my life. Through the years, particularly in pastoral ministry and relating to my wife and children, I've often been challenged to use the words of this verse as a standard for conversation. Many commercial vehicles have governors, or speed controllers, that regulate how fast a vehicle can go. God's truth and the Holy Spirit have served as governors over my lips many times—and restrained me on more occasions than I can remember. Kent Hughes writes, "Offered to God on the altar, the tongue has awesome power for good."[xliii]

Sometimes I have failed miserably as an adult in my speech. At times I had to go back and apologize for something spoken inappropriately. But I've also learned to try and put my communication through a test of some basic questions:

- Is it true?
- Will it benefit or tear others down?
- Is it helpful?
- Will saying this please Jesus?

This does not mean there is never a time for confrontation, rebuke, or correction. Sometimes life demands we have tough conversations. Jesus reserved stinging, biting words for the religious leaders in His day who mistreated people under their care. The prophets denounced sin in sometimes scathing language. But in most situations, our day-by-day conversations should reflect the qualities listed by Paul in the book of Philippians: true, honorable, right, pure, lovely, admirable, excellent, and worthy of praise (Philippians 4:8, NLT).

Yes, Jesus wants to tame our tongue. Unfortunately, the availability of instant communication in the digital age has increased the difficulty of keeping our mouths tamed. Because of social media, everyone can act like an expert on any subject, people assume their opinion needs to be shared, and concepts like common decency, respect, and civility are in rare supply.

Why Purity Is so Hard to Find

For several millennia, prior to the introduction of the digital age, if a conflict emerged between two people, they had a couple of options. They could talk about it face to face, or they could write a letter. The good thing about writing is that it follows a filtering process. Your first draft comes across angry. So you rewrite it. The second one may not be much better. So you keep rewriting. You may spend days getting that letter where you think it needs to be. Then, when the telephone was introduced into homes about one hundred years ago, people had a third option: call the person and talk. From the beginning of time until twenty years ago, these were your only choices to voice a disagreement or resolve a conflict.

Young people growing up the past two decades entered a world where instant communication was normal. Email, texts, chats, Tik Toks, and Zoom meetings are suddenly the normal means of transferring information. With inventions, what became normative would have been abnormal for all of previous time. Currently, I see three major problems when it comes to practicing godliness and holiness with the development of the digital world.

1. The Availability of Immorality

Josh McDowell shocked me when, at an apologetics conference at First Baptist Church, North Spartanburg, South Carolina, he said the church is facing the single greatest threat to holiness in twenty centuries. The threat? Internet pornography. When I grew up, porn was available but largely limited to a few magazines and certain movies—the ones we did not go to see. Today, any child holding a smart phone can instantly access thousands of pornographic pictures and videos."

2. Rudeness as an Acceptable Norm

Frederick Faber said, "Kindness has converted more sinners than zeal, eloquence, or learning."[xliv] Sadly, today our world embraces crudeness, discourtesy, and incivility. This trait has even crept into the church.

3. The Removal of Margin

The inventions of electricity and the digital world removed the millennia-old practice of slowing down and stopping when it got dark. Because there is always more information, entertainment, or stimulation to put into our minds and ears, we are training ourselves to live without margin. What is margin? You know, it's the space in a book or magazine in between the edge of the page and the printed words. A book without margins is difficult to read and a mental stumbling block. Adequate margins allow our eyes to rest as we read.

Take email, for example. Culture may have trained us that we should habitually check email. I know some work environments that expect their employees to be tied to their devices even when on vacation. But just because the culture considers it a norm does not mean it is wise and healthy. Consider taking breaks from email when possible, getting off unnecessary lists, not always replying, not answering forwards, taking a 24-hour email Sabbath weekly, and not getting upset when people fail to reply.

Discipline in Purity

If we are going to walk in purity, we must embrace self-control and good habits. The book of Proverbs repeatedly emphasizes the concept of discipline.

- *"A fool despises his father's discipline, but a person who accepts correction is sensible"* (15:5, CSB).
- *"Anyone who ignores discipline despises himself, but whoever listens to correction acquires good sense"* (15:32, CSB).
- Wise parents discipline their children. They take Solomon's advice in Proverbs 29:17, *"Discipline your child, and it will bring you peace of mind and give you delight"* (CSB).

The concept of discipline isn't primarily punishment, though some is involved. To discipline is to train, like an athlete prepares her body for competition. A good writer says no to many distractions in order to sit in his chair and put words on paper. A great guitarist spends countless hours picking the strings. Discipline involves training to follow a certain path, correcting deviant behavior and keeping your sight on the goal.

Godly parents begin their parenting with the end in sight. When God entrusts a baby to a couple, He gives them about eighteen to twenty years to invest in that child. The goal, however, is not for the child to perpetually depend on his parents. The aim is to raise a responsible adult.

When my oldest turned nine, it hit me hard. He was halfway

to eighteen, which meant the time in front of us with him at home was less than what was behind. One day Hendrix and I rode in my minivan on the Clinton-Laurens highway in South Carolina. Out of the blue, I told him, "Son, for the first nine years of your life my goal was to help you be a happy child. Do you know what my goal is for the next nine years?" When he said no, I replied, "My goal is to help you become a man." Hendrix grinned from ear to ear, always eager to grow up and be independent.

We want to raise wise, responsible adults. That is why the Bible emphasizes the training of youth. It's why parents want to teach their children how to obey at a young age.

The Bible warns that the world offers many substitutes for holiness, pulling our attention and our flesh in various directions. Discipline is essential to living a godly, productive life. Learning to tame our naturalness and submit to Christ's yoke will lead to fruitful outcomes that reflect our Creator.

Questions to Consider

1. Where are you lacking discipline in your life? How can you pray to God to help remove impurities in your life?
2. In what area of your life do you need to respond to God with first-time obedience?
3. What are some ways you need to "tame the tongue" this week?

Prayer for This Week

Father, help me to accept and cherish Your discipline. Return me to the path of righteousness, so that I may give You my first-time obedience. Amen.

If you want to skip to week one of Provision, head to page 155.

PRAYER FOR PURITY

Week Two: Purity of Heart

Teaching obedience involves instruction, training, and consequences. When our kids were preschoolers, we prepared them with lots of instruction that we expected obedience. We discussed biblical examples of people who obeyed—and who disobeyed. We taught them when we called their names, they were to stop what they were doing, say "yes, ma'am" or "yes, sir," and immediately come to us. We even made games of it sometimes to see who would get to us the fastest.

When our children obeyed freely, we occasionally chose to reward them. And when disobedience occurred, punishment followed. Preschool and elementary age children aren't too young to learn that actions have consequences, both positive and negative. No, it didn't produce perfect children. But it did create an expectation of obedience within our home, and it helped them begin developing submissive wills to authority.

The Link between Obedience and Purity

Words like *obedience, godliness,* and *discipline* all relate to another biblical word: *purity.*

Jesus made an outstanding claim in the Beatitudes. As He painted a picture of His followers' character, He said, *"Blessed are the pure in heart, for they shall see God"* (Matthew 5:8, ESV). People who maintain a pure heart will receive the ability to perceive, discern, and experience the Lord in the rhythms of life.

The English word *pure* comes from the Greek *katharos,* usually translated "clean or pure," and meaning "free from the admixture or adhesion of anything that soils, adulterates, corrupts."[xlv] Matthew used it elsewhere to describe the clean linen shroud used for Jesus' body. The apostle John portrays the armies of heaven as *"dressed in the finest of pure white linen"* (Revelation 19:14, NLT) and the New Jerusalem's main street as made of "pure gold" (Revelation 21:21, NLT). You can find other instances of this word being used in 1 Timothy 1:5, 1 Peter 1:22, and Matthew 23:36.

There's a strange phenomenon that happens in public places. Go to a grocery store or shopping mall, stand for a while, and you might experience something like the following exchange. A frazzled mom tells her child to get away from the lobster case. Little Ezekiel stands in the seafood section, getting ready to pick up a nearby mop and use it to stir the lobsters in the water tank. The child completely ignores her instruction. She again says, only louder, "Ezekiel, get away from there."

Ezekiel, fixated on the lobsters, dips the mop into the water. Finally, mom proceeds with the illogical.

She counts, very loudly, "Okay, Ezekiel Buford Smith! One ... two ... THREE!" By three, most likely Zeke has put the mop down begrudgingly, turned from the display case, and taken one or two steps toward his mother—who is very good at counting. Now, Ezekiel's mother has done an excellent job training him. But what she doesn't realize is exactly what she trained him to do. She taught little Zeke that he doesn't have to obey until she counts to three. She taught him to not obey the first or second time.

God expects our first-time obedience. Biblical accounts record such behavior. When the Lord told Abraham to sacrifice his son, the Bible says the patriarch rose early the next morning, saddled his donkey, and prepared to obey. When Jesus gave Peter an instruction regarding fishing, though Peter admitted it seemed illogical, he replied, *"But if you say so, I'll let down the nets"* (Luke 5:5b, CSB). In another account, King Saul received clear instructions from the prophet to attack and completely destroy the Amalekites and all their animals. Instead, he chose to keep some of the best for himself. Samuel appeared and rebuked him for his disobedience, offering this admonition: *"Look, to obey is better than sacrifice, to pay attention is better than the fat of rams"* (1 Samuel 15:22b, CSB).

Raising children to be fruit-bearing disciples of Jesus Christ means teaching them first-time obedience—because God doesn't like to count to three.

Guarding Your Heart

"First clean the inside of the cup and the plate, that the outside also may be clean" (Matthew 23:26, ESV). Our Lord's words here drive home the reality of purity, or godliness. Living a pure life primarily deals with the inside of a person, his heart. Our culture thinks the heart is mainly about doing what feels right to you. Countless love songs advise the listener to follow his heart. Pastor John MacArthur, in his comments on the book of Proverbs, explains the heart from a biblical perspective:

The "heart" commonly refers to the mind as the center of thinking and reason (3:3; 6:21; 7:3), but also includes the emotions (15:15, 30), the will (11:20; 4:14), and thus, the whole inner being (3:5). The heart is the depository of all wisdom and the source of whatever affects speech (4:24), sight (v. 25), and conduct (vv. 26-27).[xlvi]

So you see why Solomon warned young people to guard their hearts (Proverbs 4:23, NIV). We are to vigilantly protect our heart because it *"determines the course of your life"* (Proverbs 4:23, NLT).[xlvii]

Jesus warned about what we put into our minds and spirits (Matthew 6:22-23). With modern devices that include music, podcasts, and broadcasts, I expect if Jesus said this today, He would include "your ears."

Biblical authors knew making wise choices, keeping your integrity, maximizing your God-given potential, and living a godly, holy life hinge on what goes in our hearts—and what we put into them through our eyes and ears.

The Lord Who Sanctifies You

The book of Exodus describes a significant account when the Lord laid out a pattern for His people to live godly lives. Three months after Israel walked through the Red Sea, they arrived at the wilderness of Sinai and camped in front of the mountain. God was about to initiate His covenant with the nation, giving them the basis for their self-identity. Much like the Revolutionary War and the Constitution defined the United States of America, so the crossing of the Red Sea and the Sinai Covenant defined Israel. God also provided the Ten Commandments, or Decalogue, which became a basis for their social-moral-legal order.

In some of the most picturesque language of the Old Testament, the Lord describes their relationship. Turn in your Bible to Exodus 19:4-6 to get the full picture.

The Lord told Moses to prepare for the third day, when He would come down and show Himself: *"But you shall set boundaries for the people all around"* (19:12, NASB). God even warns Moses of the penalty of death for not observing the proper boundaries. And He instructs, *"You must keep My Sabbaths, for this is a sign between Me and you throughout your generations, so that you may know that I am the Lord who sanctifies you"* (31:13b, NASB).

Here we find the name of God Jehovah-Medkoddishkem, "the Lord who sanctifies you" or "the Lord who makes you holy." Five observations jump out from this critical passage:

1. God worked on their behalf—and they knew it.

He initiated a covenant with His people. They could not save themselves apart from His deliverance. When He worked, it was obvious and undeniable. The parting of the Red Sea and the ground of the seabed instantly drying stand as perhaps the greatest miracle in the Old Testament.

So today, the gift of Jesus Christ, sent to this earth as the incarnate Son of God, living a perfect life, dying as a substitute for our sins, and rising from the dead, is without question the greatest act of God on our behalf.

2. He carried them tenderly and brought them into a relationship.

The language used is affectionate, like a parent and young child. He desires closeness with His people. The words "own possession" can be translated "special treasure." God amazingly tells them that though He owns everything in the earth, His people are His most valued possession. He then makes a conditional promise.

3. God wants His people to obey Him and be holy.

If they would obey Him, walking in this covenant, then *"you shall be to Me a kingdom of priests and a holy nation"* (19:6, ESV). Do you see how important godliness is to the Lord? At the very center of His desire to create a people for Himself, He wants them to be people of holiness."

4. He promises His presence.

Moses would later pray, *"If Your presence does not go with us, do not lead us up from here"* (Exodus 33:15b, NASB). And God knows it is as we learn to practice His presence, drawing from the life-giving power of the Spirit inside of us that we experience His producing fruit through our lives.

5. He tells them to set boundaries.

The Lord wanted borders erected to keep the people from coming up the mountain. The people were not to break through under penalty of death. The Lord took borders and boundaries seriously. When God finished His introduction to the Covenant, He then revealed the Ten Commandments and gave the people the pattern for the Tabernacle—the place He would be worshiped for the next several decades. True worship is central to walking in godliness, and the Lord wanted His people to be lifestyle worshipers. When He finished giving them careful instructions about worship, He then turned to another subject: rest.

Keeping the Sabbath Holy

In Exodus 31:12-18, the Lord completed this entire covenant section by addressing the need for rest: *"Above all you shall keep my Sabbaths, for this is a sign between me and you throughout your generations, that you may know that I, the Lord, sanctify you"* (Exodus 31:13b, ESV). He ends with an important principle: life works best when we practice Sabbath. When we stop our labors. When we stop trying and instead trust. When we rest. A healthy life requires it.

Questions to Consider

1. What does the name "the Lord who sanctifies you" mean to you? How does it play a significant role in your growth as a Christian?
2. What is sitting at the center of your heart? Is it Jesus, or have you replaced Jesus with another idol?
3. What are some spiritual boundaries you need to set in obedience to God?

Prayer for This Week

Father, You are the Lord who sanctifies me. Edge out anything in my heart that seeks to replace You. And help me to set boundaries, so that I may focus on You and only You. Amen.

If you want to skip to week two of Provision, head to page 161.

Week Three: Purity in Rest

We live in a day marked by excessive overload. The idea of balance, a key to a stable life, is often ignored and seldom rewarded. However, great achievers have often understood the necessity and benefits of slowing down.

- Henry Ford said he didn't value executives who were always in a whirlwind of activity at their desks.
- Thomas Edison went to the edge of a lake most mornings, throwing out his line without any bait. He watched the bobber for an hour to clear his mind and prepare himself to think.
- Biblical characters like Elijah, Elisha and the apostle Paul spent hours walking between villages and cities—giving them much time to think, pray, and talk.[xlviii]

Our culture, however, "glamorizes being under time pressure."[xlix] Being habitually stressed out with too much to do is often seen as a normal part of life in the twenty-first century.

The acrostic R-E-S-T helps me remember what God says to His people about living a balanced life.

R – Respect God

"The fear of the Lord is the beginning of knowledge," writes the author of Proverbs (1:7, ESV). Healthy, holy living begins with reverencing God and submitting to His Word.

E – Establish Boundaries

Henry Cloud writes in his best-selling book *Boundaries:*

> "Boundaries define us. They define what is me and what is not me. A boundary shows me where I end and someone else begins, leading me to a sense of ownership. Knowing what I am to own and take responsibility for gives me freedom."[1]

S – Simplify and Rest

Thankfully, though we can draw unchanging principles from Exodus, one significant difference exists between then and now. We don't approach God through Moses or Mt. Sinai anymore. Centuries later, the author of Hebrews wrote to Jewish believers, *"For you have not come to a mountain that can be touched and to a blazing fire, and to darkness and gloom and whirlwind … But you have come to Mount Zion and to the city of the living God, the heavenly Jerusalem … and to Jesus, the mediator of a new covenant …"* (Hebrews 12:18, 22, 24, NASB).

Earlier in the same book, the author explained, *"We have been sanctified through the offering of the body of Jesus Christ once for all time"* (10:10, NASB). Our purity and holiness don't start by controlling our actions, thoughts, or words. We first receive holiness from God when we put our trust in His Son Jesus Christ for the forgiveness of our sins.

There's something called positional holiness. I stop trying to get to God on my own, repent of my sins and my sinful nature, and turn to Christ in faith. The Father makes me His child legally, permanently, and positionally, giving—or imputing—Christ's holiness to me. So my permanent record now says, "Rhett is holy." Praise God for that.

The Pharisees focused on following man-made rules, attempting to control external behavior. But they missed the Source of all holiness and goodness. When you become a Christian, God puts His life-giving Spirit inside of you, and His presence is the One who enables you to live a godly life day in and day out. The first step in leading our children to live godly lives is to introduce them to the Giver of life through a relationship with Jesus Christ.

The author of Hebrews picked up this Old Testament image of rest and Sabbath to illustrate how our right-standing with God comes only through Christ: *"There remains a Sabbath rest for the people of God, for whoever has entered God's rest has also rested from his works as God did from His. Let us therefore strive to enter that rest"* (4:9-11, ESV). He's not talking about working hard to earn your salvation. He is saying that when we come to Jesus, we can rest from our efforts to save ourselves, and instead, receive His forgiveness and holiness.

T – Train with Good Habits

As a believer, I want my life to reflect my position. I want my walking to reflect my standing. I can never do anything to make God love me more nor to cause Him to take away His positional purity from my account. However, every day I make choices that move my behavior either closer to or further from practical holiness.

What a Sabbath Involves

Unfortunately, we live in an era that embraces bad habits. And perhaps none of those habits may be worse than the one of Lightning McQueen from the movie *Cars*—speed.

"What is the greatest threat to the modern family?" This question was asked to Dr. James Dobson three decades ago. His answer was surprising. He didn't say the threat of marital infidelity, greed, pornography, or the negative influences of the entertainment culture. He simply said, "The greatest threat is the speed of life in Western society."

God is honored and our lives work better when we practice the biblical concept of Sabbath. And Sabbath involves two things: **worship and rest.**

However, in our day, speed is the norm. In our fast-paced world, Christians need to recover the practice of Sabbath-rest if we're to live balanced lives. In order for life to work at its optimum degree, believers need to incorporate worship and rest into our lives weekly. Our Creator designed life to function better when we take time on a weekly basis to worship with other believers and slowdown from life's busy pace.

The Bible commands us to come together regularly with our church family under the preaching of the Word, the singing of spiritual songs, the lifting of prayers, and the encouragement of the saints. As a pastor, I see the marginalization of the Lord's Day increasing. People go to the movies or ballgames on Saturday night, so they skip church on Sunday. They have a rough week, so they sleep in. One child is sick, so no one in the family goes to church.

My parents once taught me how much they valued our going to church on the Lord's Day. I participated in a neighborhood swim team, and that summer weekend they planned for a lock-in on Saturday evening at our pool. I assumed I would attend. To my surprise, my mother said, "No, Son, you won't be going. We're Christians, and the Bible says that Sunday is the Lord's Day. We worship God on Sunday morning with other believers. That takes priority over a lock-in." I walked to the back of our yard, sat under an apple tree, and pouted. In my disappointment, I pondered what Mom said and how important my parents took weekly engagement with our local congregation.

Just because that was my experience doesn't make it right or wrong. You may choose to let your child go to a Saturday night lock-in. But the point is my parents had a conviction—as have Christians historically—that Sunday belonged to the Lord. Looking back, I don't think they were legalistic about church-going, and I appreciate their consistency. They taught me that our family had a simple but strong conviction: Sunday is the Lord's Day, and we meet with other believers on His day.

Albert Mohler, president of the Southern Baptist Theological Seminary, writes:

We are to make it a priority of our lives that on this day we will be with God's people, we will be with the redeemed, we will be with the saints, and we will gather together to prepare for eternity, to be confronted with the Word of God, to edify one another and to yearn for that eternal rest which is promised unto us by the grace and mercy of God.[li]

The discipline of church attendance trains our families in the ways of the Lord, teaches our children how to listen to God's Word, encourages other believers to pray together, and shows them that our lives are a part of something much bigger than our personal pleasure. My wife and I found much help when our children were preschoolers from Robbie Castleman's *Parenting in the Pew: Guiding Your Children into the Joy of Worship*. We highly recommend it to you.

On Thursdays, I ask God to keep us pure in mind, body, and spirit.

Questions to Consider

1. Have you prioritized going to church on a weekly basis? Why or why not?

2. What are some ways you can incorporate rest into your life?

3. What are some ways you see "speed" edging the Lord out of your life?

Prayer for This Week

Father, You are the Lord of the Sabbath. May I prioritize rest and worship. Help me to realize areas in my life where speed hinders my relationship with You. Amen.

If you want to skip to week three of Provision, head to page 169.

Week Four: Purity in Remembrance and Reclaiming

In Psalm 78, Asaph, one of the songwriters under David, retold part of the Jewish people's history from Egyptian slavery to the Davidic reign. Recalling highs and lows of their history, he remembers:

- The plagues under Moses
- The Red Sea crossing
- The pillar of fire in the wilderness
- God's provision of manna and quail
- Their refusal to trust God in the desert
- The conquering of the Promised Land
- The loss of the Ark of the Covenant
- And the establishment of David's kingdom

Why does the Bible spill so much ink on past events? Because the author knew the people would be tempted to forget their history, forget what God had done, and ignore the Lord altogether. Remembering correctly is a fundamental part of being a faithful believer. And good parenting involves passing on correct knowledge worth remembering.

Remembering as a Family

Have you ever heard of an Ebenezer stone? Perhaps you have in a worship song or during a Bible study. An Ebenezer stone was a structure—often a formation or piles of stones—that helped the Israelites to remember important events. It would help them to recall where they came from, and whose they were (the Lord's).

In the same way, we can remember who our family belongs to and how God delivered us from "the desert," from our enemies—much like the Israelites.

Find ways to create an Ebenezer as a family. It doesn't necessarily have to be a physical structure like the piles of stones in the Old Testament. But collaborate and discuss ways to recall the Lord's goodness in your life and the lives of your family members.

Reclaiming the Family Table

As mentioned in a previous chapter, one of the best ways to practice this remembering is reclaiming the family table, when the household sits around a table together and eats a meal. No cellphones or tablets. No TV. No rushed agenda.

I realize we can't do this every day. But I urge you to resist the cultural norm of not making regular sit-down mealtimes a priority. Mealtimes offer rich opportunities for influencing the next generation.

Varying levels of communication exist. One level asks, *What did you do?* Deeper than that is, *What do you think?* Even further is, *How did that make you feel?* Or *What do you wish?* Work at having conversations that don't only stay on the first level.

Our oldest son loves asking what-if questions. He regularly asks us probing things like, "What would you do with a million dollars? If you could travel anywhere in the world for one year, where would you go? If you had only one superpower, what would you choose?" Engaging in such discussions builds family cohesiveness and offers opportunities to share wisdom.

We can't keep society from speeding up, embracing immorality, or driving off a cliff. We can, however, choose to lead our families along a different path, embracing Paul's challenge in Romans 12, *"Don't let the world around you squeeze you into its own mould, but let God re-mould your minds from within, so that you may prove in practice that the plan of God for you is good, meets all His demands and moves towards the goal of true maturity"* (v.2, JBP).

On Thursdays, I ask the Lord to help us walk in purity. With this foundation, we can confidently ask God for the next P in our prayer-pattern: provision. And the Lord has more than 10,000 ways to supply for His children.

Questions to Consider

1. What are some Ebenezers you can remember as a family, about God's goodness in your lives?
2. How do you plan to "reclaim the table" this week?
3. This month, how do you intend to "walk in purity," personally and as a family?

Prayer for This Week

Father, help me to reclaim my table and remember Your goodness in my life. May I help future generations to see Your goodness throughout the ages. Amen.

If you want to skip to week four of Provision, head to page 177.

PRAYER POINTS FOR PURITY

1. Ask the Lord to mature us in taming our tongues, choosing to use this communication test:
   - Is it true?
   - Will it benefit or tear down others?
   - Will saying this please the Lord?

2. Help our family to embrace a disciplined lifestyle:
   - Self-controlled and practicing good habits.
   - Correcting wrong behavior and providing proper training.
   - Practicing appropriate obedience and respect for authority.

3. Pray that we will value the biblical concept of REST:
   - Respecting the Lord.
   - Establishing boundaries.
   - Simplifying our lives and resting.
   - Training with good habits.

4. Help us resist the cultural norm of burnout and, instead, build healthy margin into our lives.
   - Ask for wisdom to know how to not be sucked into the culture's bad habits.
   - Pray for the discipline to say no to unhealthy habits and yes to protective boundaries.
   - Help us to build habits that produce life.

PRAYER FOR PROVISION

Week One: Before We Ask Him

God provided in an unusual way. The summer following college graduation, while preparing for seminary, I worked at a church as a children and youth intern. God would challenge me in the coming years to learn to trust Him financially step-by-step. He created an experience that summer to prove Himself faithful and teach me that I could trust Him to provide for my present and future needs.

One Wednesday afternoon I visited Crossway bookstore in Greenville, South Carolina. Browsing through the shelves, I sensed the quiet, consistent nudge of God: *Buy these five books and give them to the man you disciple.* I knew that voice. And I questioned that voice. As a young man on the way to seminary, I didn't have money to squander. I prayed, *Lord, You know I don't have money to spare. But if this is You, I will trust You.* As an act of obedience, I purchased the books for $48.

Later, feeling foolish and questioning my experience, I went to church and walked into my office. Stan, the custodian, came in and presented an envelope. I asked, "Who is this from?"

He answered, "I don't know."

I said, "What do you mean, you don't know?"

"That's what they told me to tell you, I don't know."

Stan left, and I opened the envelope. Inside was a note that read, *God knows our needs before we ask Him.* The note, unsigned, included a fifty-dollar bill.

I sat there, stunned. God saw me. God guided me. I heard from Him. And He was real. I could step out in faith and trust Him to be faithful. God was teaching me the reality of Luke 6:38: *"Give, and it will be given to you. A good measure, pressed down, shaken together and running over, will be poured into your lap"* (NIV).

That word from God changed my life. To this day I keep that unsigned note as a reminder of God's faithfulness. The experience became a mental altar for me. In the Old Testament, when people encountered God in a significant way, they often stopped and built an altar to the Lord. Henry and Richard Blackaby explain: "Often, people in the Old Testament set up stone markers or altars as reminders of their encounters with God. Places like Bethel (house of God) and Rehoboth (room) became reminders of God's great activity in the midst of His people."[lii]

Through the years, I wondered about the giver of the money. That afternoon, I imagined the Holy Spirit stirring in her, challenging, *Give Rhett Wilson $50 today.* What if she ignored the Spirit's prompting? What if she said, "I will do that later this week, Lord." What if she had dismissed it as foolishness? I still don't know who gave that money. But she listened to the Lord. She obeyed. And God used her to administer His grace and provision to me in a way that I have never forgotten.

I return to this mental altar time after time, reminding me of the Lord my Provider. I can look to the Lord first—not the bank account. God knows my needs before I ask Him.

Unexpected Encouragement

At the time, I was just a few weeks away from moving to Louisville, Kentucky, to begin my seminary career. Because I attended a college less than one hour from home, going to graduate school would be the first time in my life I was really out on my own. Through the previous year, step-by-step I concluded that I thought the Lord wanted me to go pursue a seminary degree after graduation. Like most students determining what to do with their lives, it had been a complicated process of considering, praying, and getting advice.

One Saturday morning, the telephone woke me up at 9:30 a.m.—still early for a college student. The caller's South African-English brogue loudly greeted me that morning on my answering machine, as I heard, "Rhett, this is Don Wilton, pastor of First Baptist Church of Spartanburg. I heard about you, and I want you to come to my office sometime and let's talk." For a twenty-two-year-old to receive an unexpected call from the man who would be known as Billy Graham's pastor, I was stunned.

A few weeks later, I drove to Spartanburg and sat down with the amiable Dr. Wilton. He encouraged me and challenged me to trust God and take the next step. He also offered advice

I have never forgotten. Citing the call of Abram in Genesis 12, he read Abram's response, recorded in the book of Hebrews: *"By faith Abraham, when called to go to a place he would later receive as his inheritance, obeyed and went, even though he did not know where he was going"* (11:8, NIV). Don then told a story about a couple with children who sensed the Lord telling them to leave their current place in life and go to seminary: "I asked them why they have not gone, and they told me, 'Well, we want to first find schools for the children, a place to live, and get all of the details worked out.' I said, 'So, in other words, you are waiting to get all of your ducks in a row.' And they replied, 'Yes.' Rhett, then I told them with a twinkle in my eye, 'You know, I've read the Bible from cover to cover several times. And do you know, there are no ducks in the Bible?'"

The pastor's humor drives home a point: many times, God challenges us to take action before knowing how the details will fall into place. As aforementioned in chapter four, Charles Stanley's life-principle rings true, "Obey God, and leave all the consequences to Him."

In the months following my meeting with Dr. Wilton, concluding that obedience to God meant going to seminary in the fall, I determined to obey Him, leaving the consequences to Him. One of those *consequences* was needing money to attend. My parents did not have the resources to continue paying for my education, and I did not know how to get all of the ducks in a row. Looking back more than a quarter of a century, I guess it was youthful ignorance combined with gritty faith. I just trusted that the God who was calling me would provide.

The fifty-dollar bookstore provision in the middle of that summer served as a significant confirmation to me at the time to keep trusting the Lord and to keep moving forward. Then, about ten days before I planned to make the 400-mile move to Louisville, my mother received an unexpected note in the mail from a relative who was aware of my plans to go to school. The generous benefactor had sent a check for $10,000 to the school to be deposited into my account and used as needed. The gift was completely unsolicited, and to my remembrance I had not had any conversations with the relative about my plans. This provision was an incredible help the next two years in paying for tuition and school-related expenses.

But the story does not end there. God is always one step ahead of us. While studying as a full-time student and also working to meet basic needs, after two years the 10K supply ran out. The same month that money was gone, my mother received a phone call from a lady in North Carolina. Her daughter and I sang in college choir together. We had not spoken since college graduation—remember this was pre-social media. Her mother served on a committee at a small church who had a scholarship fund for seminary students. However, they did not know any. Her daughter said, "Mom, I think Rhett Wilson from college choir is now in seminary." Her mother contacted the school to find my home contact information. She told my mother they would mail an application to me. Several weeks later, I filled it out and sent it back, having no idea what amount to expect. To my shock and surprise, the next year, that small Presbyterian church sent $5000 to me, which helped me finish my seminary career.

As a father of three young adult children in college, I continue learning to look to God as my Source and trusting Him for the needs of five people—not just one. The lesson God began teaching me in that bookstore applies just as much now as it did then. God is the Provider for my family. He can be trusted. We can risk some of what we have today and trust Him for what we need tomorrow.

Questions to Consider

1. How has the Lord provided for you specifically in the past?
2. Who might need your unexpected encouragement as they struggle through life?
3. Where do you need to be reminded that God is always one step ahead of you?

Prayer for this Week

Father, thank You for knowing my needs before I even ask for them. As you ask me to walk with You, enable me to be governed by faith – not fear. Amen.

If you want to skip to week one of Presence, head to page 185.

PRAYER FOR PROVISION

Week Two: Mount Moriah

Stepping Out and Trusting Him

A number of years ago our family believed God was leading me to take a huge step of faith and resign from my current position without a job—trusting Him for the next step. On an October prayer retreat at Ridgecrest Conference Center, I stretched out face down on the cement slab of a shelter my children used during summer camp. I prayed, *Lord, I have no idea how I am going to provide for my family. Christmas is coming, and I will need money for Christmas presents for them. But, Father, if I know you are leading us, I will step out and obey You.* The Father confirmed that day to both my wife and me to move forward. I resigned that afternoon. A scary move.

One month later, Chris, one of my best friends, took me out to lunch. I had told no one my fear of not having money for Christmas presents. Leaving the restaurant, he followed me to my car, put his hand on my shoulder, and said, "Rhett, I

believe you have obeyed the Lord, and I respect you for stepping out in faith. I know that Christmas is coming, and you
want to bless your children. I just want you to know that I
support you as you follow God." He handed me a sealed envelope filled with $1000 in cash.

As we stepped out in faith that season, the Lord eventually
led us to be part of serving in another church. Our former
church graciously compensated me for several months after
my resignation. By the time that provision ended, I was working in my new position.

Life continues to hold challenges for my wife and me to
trust in God's financial provision. We work. We give. We try
to spend wisely. We trust Him to care for us. And we continue
learning the lesson that we can depend on the God who sees
us and knows our needs, both today and tomorrow.

The Bible is replete with accounts of God's providing for His
people, many times at the eleventh hour. Years ago, I attended
a pastors' conference led by Henry Blackaby, who shared that
in all his years of life and ministry, God had never been late in
His provision. Then he added, "And my wife, Marilyn, who is
an exact opposite of me in many ways, would be quick to add,
'And seldom early!'"

Many times in life we find ourselves with our backs against
the wall, needing help. The supply we ask God for is not limited to finances. It could be a job, a place to live, a vehicle, a
spouse, or a friend. The summer after my first year in college,
I worked as an intern for children and youth at Welcome Baptist Church. It was a fantastic experience, and I made many
valuable relationships with those families. The next year in

April, I was walking across my college campus in Clinton, South Carolina, almost fifty miles from Welcome Church. As I crossed South Adair Street, the main street intersecting the campus, I noticed a long car suddenly stop and pull into a nearby parking spot. The door opened, and I heard a familiar voice yell, "Rhett Wilson!" To my surprise, out stepped Betty Ragan, a young senior adult from Welcome who helped me a lot the previous summer on church outings. She and her sister were visiting someone in Clinton, and they just happened to be driving down South Adair at the exact moment I was walking by.

Betty spotted me and told her sister, "Stop the car!" She asked me if I had any plans of employment for the summer. I had none. She asked, "Would you like to come back to Welcome?" I responded affirmatively, and she said with a wink, "I'll see what I can do." Within days, the church officially contacted me and extended the job for the summer. I ended up working at Welcome for three summers in college, and to this day still keep up with some of these fine people.

The Mountain of Supply

As a college student I picked up Kay Arthur's study *LORD, I Want to Know You.* In it, she teaches the reader many of God's names. I cut some of my theological teeth learning to revere God through these self-acclaimed words. The book of Proverbs says, *"The name of the LORD is a strong tower; the righteous runs into it and is safe"* (Proverbs 18:10, NASB). And the psalmist wrote, *"Some trust in chariots and some in horses, but we trust in the name of the LORD our God"* (Psalm 20:7, ESV).

It doesn't mean that in warfare they didn't use the day's available weapons, but it does mean their ultimate trust, boast, or confidence was in God.

Over and over, the psalmist writes of boasting in the name of the Lord: *"I bow down toward your holy temple and give thanks to your name for your steadfast love and your faithfulness, for you have exalted above all things your name and your word"* (Psalm 138:2, ESV). I love how the New Living Translation states that last phrase: *"your promises are backed by all the honor of your name."* God's names reveal His character. They show us reasons to trust Him, expectations of the covenant relationship. They remind us of who He is.

In the familiar text of Genesis 22, God reveals His name as Jehovah-Jireh, meaning "The LORD will provide." God tests His servant Abraham, asking him to take his promised son Isaac to the region of Moriah and sacrifice him on a mountain. Through great struggle, the father of faith prepares to obey. The patriarch knows the Lord has sworn to give him many descendants through Isaac. The eleventh chapter of Hebrews gives insight into Abraham's thinking: *"He considered that God was able even to raise him from the dead"* (11:19a, ESV). Old Abe knew the Lord's Word, character, and promises were absolutely trustworthy. So he reckoned that if God told him to sacrifice Isaac, then God planned to raise him back to life. That is faith in action.

A beautiful moment occurs as father and son make their way up the mountain. The Bible says, *"So Abraham placed the wood for the burnt offering on Isaac's shoulders, while he himself carried the fire and the knife"* (Genesis 22:6a, NLT). As Isaac walks up Mount Moriah, he had no way of knowing that he was a type—a symbol—of another one centuries later who would walk toward a hill of sacrifice with a wooden cross on His back. Isaac realizes there is no animal and he asks, *"Where is the lamb?"* (22:7, NIV). His father's response reveals the depth and confidence of his faith. *"God will provide for himself the lamb for a burnt offering"* (22:8, ESV).

God will provide for His will to be done. Every time.

When they reach the top of the mountain to the place of sacrifice, the father binds the son. It's worth noting that Isaac is no small child at this point. It is more likely he is an older teenager or young adult who could have easily overpowered the aging father. Many times, I like to imagine what is in-between the lines of our Bibles—the parts that did not get recorded. Imagine that moment, when Abraham, with tears in his eyes, looks directly into Isaac's, the son of promise, and says, "My beloved son, God has told me to do something very difficult."

The fact that Isaac submitted himself to the process reveals the depth of trust he had in his earthly father and the extent of discipleship that had passed between them. Isaac knew his father walked with God. He knew Abraham was trustworthy. And Isaac did his own considering or reckoning. He knew his God and his earthly father were both trustworthy. So he literally put it all on the altar.

God has provision. Or pro-vision. He sees. He sees beforehand. He sees ahead. He knows what is coming. And in seeing, He provides for the need. Nothing surprises Him.

English preacher and author Thomas Watson wrote in the 1600s, "God is to be trusted when His providences seem to run contrary to His promises . . ." The name Jehovah-Jireh reminds us that God sees, He knows, and He is faithful.

The climax occurs when Abraham raises the knife to slay his son and suddenly, a voice from heaven calls out, *"Abraham, Abraham!' And he said, 'Here I am.' He said, 'Do not lay your hand on the boy or do anything to him, for now I know that you fear God'"* (Genesis 22:11b-12a, ESV). Abraham looks up and sees a ram behind him caught by his thorns in a thicket.

Terry Akrill said, "Time is God's domain ... Sometimes God likes to do things ten seconds before midnight."[liii] Abraham and Isaac sacrifice the animal and worship the Lord. They call that place Jehovah-Jireh, which is often translated "The Lord will provide." The Hebrew word *Jireh* means "to see, observe, watch, or consider." It reminds us of God's provision. In seeing ahead of time, He is able to provide, supply, and sometimes surprise.

It's worth noting, that though the Lord is able to do anything, and His special provisions make wonderful testimonies, another means of supply should be celebrated as well. God's normal, routine, year-in and year-out way of providing for us most of the time is by the wonderful four-letter word *WORK*. From the beginning of humanity, He planned for people to use their skills and interests to produce meaningful, helpful, and profitable work. Work is not a curse; it's a blessing. Yes, there are times when God backs us into a Red Sea in order to demonstrate His power. But He does not want us depending daily on a miracle or the government or our rich uncle Louie to pay our bills and meet our needs. With few exceptions, He made us to embrace our unique designs and engage in making a living. We can discover who we are and why we are here and enjoy making a difference in this world—creating, baking, building, or fixing.

On Fridays, I ask the Lord to provide for my family.

Questions to Consider

1. Where might the Lord be challenging you to step out into the unknown, trusting Him?
2. Where are you tempted to run for your provision instead of the Lord?
3. What do you need to surrender today on your own Mount Moriah?

Prayer for this Week

Father, I rejoice in the way You faithfully displayed Your supply in the account of Abraham and Isaac. Remind me to live a surrendered life, holding things loosely, trusting You to meet the needs in my life. Amen.

If you want to skip to week two of Presence, head to page 193.

Week Three: Praying for Rain

God's Pro-Vision

Note the similarities between the words *provide, provision,* and *providence* and consider what they teach you about God's ability towards you and your family. The word provision includes the prefix *pro* and the word *vision.* Literally it means being able to see ahead of time. God has pro-vision. His sight is not limited to what you and I can see. Nothing catches Him by surprise. And He is able to put things in place before we ever know of our need. Another similar word is *providence.* See within those letters the word *provide.* God is able to work things out in order to provide for His will and glory and our good.

Pastor Tony Evans writes about God's providence:

> God is a God of intersections. He connects things that don't look connectable. He twists things that appear set in stone. He maneuvers through the maze of what appears to be un-

related occurrences … God always has a plan in play."[liv]

But sometimes these divine intersections take place when it seems pitch black outside.

My family and I found ourselves at one of those unexpected moments about twelve years ago. We were so discouraged. Why did our prayers keep going unanswered?

Three years earlier while attending Discipleship Week at Ridgecrest Conference Center, my wife and I believed the Lord wanted us to go home, sell our house, and trust Him for the next step. Though we were happy with our house, in one month we had a For Sale sign in the yard.

Nine months later we sold our home and began renting a small but livable house owned by some friends. The house was a second one they called "the barn" and was used on their property for storage. We moved from the city to the country and from 1400 square feet to what felt like far less. The barn was on 100 acres, and we thought it would be fun for the kids to roam outdoors for the summer months. We were sure we would only be there for a short while.

As the months rolled along, we came close to purchasing three different houses. The first house was a long, spacious brick ranch on Southdale Drive. It came with a wooded lot of almost two acres, perfect for our three children to enjoy. I could envision this place being a home for our family. The house needed a lot of extra work done to it, which we could not afford to do and pay near the asking price of $160,000. After making several low offers on the house, we finally gave up that dream and walked away.

As we continued house-hunting, door after door closed. The poor national economy in the fall of 2008 did not help. Almost one year after moving into the barn, we tried to purchase a second home adjacent to a large property owned by some of our best friends. We envisioned our children living next to theirs, playing in creeks, hiking through woods, and enjoying our next-door-neighbors.

The house needed a lot of work and required a reconstruction loan. Due to the poor economy, banks were not giving those types of loans. More than one banker told me, "If you had walked in here six months ago, we could have written a loan on the spot."

We finally stopped trying after seven banks turned us down. Disappointed, we walked away from that dream. Several months later we found a great house on a lake and made an offer only to find out the realtor sold it right out from under us the same day to one of his friends.

After the third house did not work out, we were both very discouraged. We had all kinds of questions and were very confused. I asked my wife, "Why do we keep hitting closed doors? Have we missed something? Are we supposed to move away? What is God doing?"

At the end of that week, we ate supper with three couples. That night we spent an hour or so in prayer together. They all knew how Tracey and I were struggling. In the middle of the time of prayer, one man boldly prayed, "Lord, give the Wilsons specific, clear direction in the next seven days." The other people in the room agreed with him, and they continued to pray in like manner—asking for revelation and breakthrough in the next seven days.

Then our friend Jay prayed, "Father, in 1 Kings 18, Elijah prayed for rain seven times."

Turning to the other couples, he said, "I believe we need to fast and pray the next seven days for the Wilsons." We all left that night with a stirring expectation that the Lord would work during the next seven days.

When Monday rolled around, Jay had everyone organized to fast and pray. Each one took a different twenty-four-hour period, each watch going from 12 a.m. to 12 a.m. Tracey and I were very humbled by their gift of love. Every day we received calls or emails from each of them saying things like, "I am on my watch today praying for you."

The first day of the fast, I checked a foreclosure website for our area. I noticed that the first house we almost purchased on Southdale Drive was listed, but under contract. The house had sat empty in the eighteen months since we withdrew our offer. Instead of asking $160,000, their price was $94,000.

The seventh day came and went without any seemingly significant breakthrough. I was accepting that even though God had not intervened dramatically, it was okay, and He was worthy of our trust. That Sunday morning I led our church in song, reminding us that God is always aware of our circumstances.

The day after the prayer vigil ended, I looked again at the foreclosure site. During our seven-day fast, the contract on Southdale fell through. Even better, on day six of the fast, the house was re-listed at a lower price of $86,900.

I quickly called to inquire of the realtor. Within one week

we had a contract on the house. My wife's father spent three months doing a major renovation of the house. With excitement we picked out honey-oak cabinets, beige shaggy carpet for the den and bedrooms, and new dark architectural shingles for the roof. My wife selected many colors for the walls, including shades of blue for the boys' room and pink and purple for our daughter's. The house received polished wood floors, a new HVAC system, and a renovated kitchen, complete with stainless steel appliances. The total cost of the house with all the new renovations was less than the original asking price of the un-renovated house two years earlier.

For eight years, what a joy it was to watch our children build forts and climb trees in that wooded lot, hold birthday parties in the backyard, and see children run and play baseball, soccer, and capture the flag. The house now contains precious memories involving Christmas trees and fall pumpkins, good-night kisses and hugs, family devotions, Saturday morning pancake breakfasts, and movie nights in the den. Our youngest son even got on his knees with his father and brother on that shaggy beige carpet in his bedroom one night to ask Jesus Christ to forgive him of his sins and make him His son.

The house on Southdale became a home for our family. Some things in life are worth the wait.

When Elijah prayed for rain, as Jay referenced, he assumed an unusual position. For three years, at God's decree, a famine consumed the land. The prophet knew it would not rain again until the Lord allowed it, and Elijah kept looking to Him for provision. After a miraculous intervention of God vindicating his name at Mount Carmel, Elijah believed it was time for rain. He climbed the mountain with his servant, and the Bible says he *"bent down to the ground and put his face between his knees"* (1 Kings 18:42b, NIV). That may look like a strange prayer position. But a Jew of his time would understand that was a position that women took when they were in labor. They didn't use stirrups or birthing beds. They crouched down and systematically began to push. And push. And push. And push—until finally a delivery occurred.

God revealed to His servant that rain would come, but Elijah had to pray that miracle into reality. So he began laboring in prayer. Seven times he asked his servant to walk over toward the sea and look for a rain cloud. Six times the servant returned seeing nothing. How easy it would have been to give up praying after time three, or four, or five. Many times we give up during the in-between of the promise or dream and the fulfillment. When no rain clouds appear after three years of drought and everything in our circumstances tells us otherwise, the natural reaction is quitting.

But not Elijah. Had he quit, he may have "defaulted on the promise and forfeited the miracle. But Elijah prayed through, and God came through."[lv] Though the Lord sent the miracle, He chose to release it through a human instrument who prayed. The seventh time, the servant noticed a small raincloud forming in the sky. And that was all the confirmation the prophet needed. He knew the baby was about to be born. Not only did it rain. It poured and poured and poured, even making it impossible for chariots to run.

Don't stop praying.

Questions to Consider

1. How have you seen God intersect circumstances, people, and opportunities before?
2. What do the words *provide, provision,* and *providence* remind you about the ability of the Lord to care for you and your family?
3. How does the story of Elijah's praying for rain encourage and challenge you in praying for your children and grandchildren?

Prayer for this Week

Father, we live in a society that loves instant gratification. Help me to embrace the long-term view in life. May I be faithful to not stop praying, partnering with You in birthing your wonders in this world. Amen.

If you want to skip to week three of Presence, head to page 199.

Week Four: Manna

When God Sends Manna

Steve Farrar wrote a wonderful, practical book about the provisions of God called *Manna: When You're Out of Options, God Will Provide.* I highly recommend it to you. During a desert experience in my own life, I picked it up, read it several times, and have been giving copies of it away ever since. Farrar defines providence as "God's detailed, purposeful, massive, daily, and continual provision for His people." He writes, "No matter where you are in life, no matter how dark your present circumstances, you can stand on the providence of God."[lvi]

Two million Israelites followed Moses out of Egypt into the wilderness. Every day they would need food and water. No sane pastor would envy Moses for his leadership responsibility. These former slaves operated with a mindset of fear and blame rather than abundance and responsibility. The Lord had to put them into the school of the desert in order to learn to live in new ways, in dependence upon Him.

With no grocery stores or markets, they needed a massive provision. And they needed it daily. Enter manna. Every morning, this bread from heaven appeared outside of their tents—just enough for each person to have one day's supply. The Lord gave instructions for each person to gather an omer of manna, the equivalent of six pints. One author explains that for two million people, that required twelve million pints, which equals nine million pounds every morning: "Today that amount of manna would require ten trains, each having thirty cars, and each car carrying fifteen tons—for a single day's supply."[lvii]

Jesus, centuries later, likely alluded to this daily provision of manna when He taught His disciples to pray, *"Give us today our daily bread"* (Matthew 6:11, NIV). In the Bible, bread not only symbolizes physical food, but spiritual food. Jesus Christ is called the Bread of Life, and the Word of God is considered spiritual bread. He once declared, *"Man shall not live on bread alone, but on every word that comes from the mouth of God"* (Matthew 4:4, NIV).

Elisabeth Elliot, well-known and revered twentieth-century Christian, author, and Bible teacher, called her own spiritual journal her "Omer of Manna." What an appropriate title. In a spiritual journal we record the daily bread God gives us through His Word.

Write it Down

How easily we do forget! I had to accept several years ago that

I was wired mentally like an absent-minded professor. I can stand up from my desk with the intention of doing one particular thing at the other end of the house. By the time I walk from one end of the house to the next, I have forgotten that thing. As a pastor, I know that I do not remember everything that I hear through my ears. A notepad close-at-hand often assists the filing cabinet of our brains. Adrian Rogers once said that *the weakest pen is greater than the strongest mind.* How true.

As important as it is to write down tasks like "I need to call Jim back" or "go look at shelves at Lowes" or "send Aunt Betsy a birthday card," how much more important it is for us to write down things that the Lord gives us.

For years I have practiced keeping a spiritual journal. However, my journal is no fancy endeavor. At any given time I have one three-ring binder that includes a spiral notebook. I keep it handy for jotting down Bible verses, prayers, quotations, or guidance from the Holy Spirit that I come across during my times of Bible meditation, reading for spiritual development, and prayer times.

God speaks in a myriad of ways. The active listener learns to write down things that we believe come from the Lord to us. However, once again, I find it easy to forget even those spiritual lessons. The Lord can grab my attention through a sermon, book, or time of prayer—only for me to forget it a few days later.

While going through the discipleship workbook *Masterlife* by Avery Willis, I learned a valuable lesson to assist me to not forget. Willis recommends that once a month we take some time to stop and review our spiritual journal from the previous

30 days. Were there any Bible passages that especially encouraged us? Was there a specific answer to prayer? Was there a new prayer-focus? Was there a promise we claimed? Did the Spirit of God impress something specific on us during our prayer time? Was there a directive or a step of obedience we intended to take?

When God prepared His people to cross into the Promised Land, He exhorted them about the importance of remembering His words and instructions: *"They are not just idle words for you—they are your life. By them you will live long in the land you are crossing the Jordan to possess"* (Deuteronomy 32:47, NIV).

As easy as it is to forget—even important things—this practice helps us to remember. The Bible is replete with instructions to remember what God has said and not forget. If we forget, we may not obey and experience God's best. We live in a day when many people remember incorrectly, throwing off God's Word and His values. Remembering correctly helps us to expect Him to be faithful today.

Take the Risk

Moses expected God to be faithful. So did Abigail.

While in the middle of writing this chapter one Friday afternoon, I received a phone call from my buddy Greg, a former colleague at the Billy Graham Evangelistic Association. He said, "I just wanted to call you and share a praise of how God has worked in our lives." His oldest of three daughters is a junior at a nearby university. The family had stretched themselves about as far as they could her first three years financing her education. A few months ago, Greg had told her, "Honey,

I just don't know if we can responsibly make this happen another year without taking out massive loans." Greg's daughter is a great student and has proven her worth at the university, where she serves as an ambassador. She is also very involved in campus ministry, including traveling to churches some weekends to lead worship and youth retreats.

One of her campus ministry leaders connected her with one of the school's vice presidents. She laid her cards on the table, told him her story, and asked if there was any financial assistance the school could provide. Though the administrator made no promises, several months later he called her to come to his office. There, he told her that they valued her presence on campus, believed in her future, and would be offering her a full-ride for her senior year. Greg wept with gratitude as he testified over the phone to me of the Lord's faithful provision.

Reflecting on Greg's testimony about his daughter, I thought, *What a tremendous story.* It certainly speaks of God's Jehovah-Jireh providence-provision. But it also reveals her diligence to do all she could do to be excellent, earning a good reputation on campus. And it speaks of Abigail's willingness to go to the person with the resources and simply ask. Jack Canfield, in his enormously popular book *The Success Principles,* shares that one of life's most valuable lessons is learning to not be afraid to ask: "Don't assume that you are going to get a no. Take the risk to ask for whatever you need and want. If they say no, you are no worse off than when you started."[lviii]

Sometimes providence intersects at the crossroads of our doing everything we know to do while trusting God to do everything that only He can do.

Our children will face a myriad of needs in their lives. On Fridays, I ask God to provide for my family. I repeatedly pray the words "provision, provide, and providence" when I pray for my kids. Ask God to give your family the relationships, opportunities, environments, and resources they need for their development, satisfaction, and fruitfulness. He has all the resources, so ask Him.

As we experience His provision again and again, we are ready to then ask for even more blessings—His prosperity.

Questions to Consider

1. What area of life do you need to ask God for His provision?
2. How are you feeding yourself daily with God's living, written bread? How can you model for your children to feed themselves daily with spiritual food?
3. Where do you need to take a risk and trust the Lord?

Prayer for this Week

Father, You are the owner of every resource and the source of endless supply. Even in life's desert seasons, You are able to care for Your own. Help me to lean on You daily for Your constant endowments. Amen.

If you want to skip to week four of Presence, head to page 207.

PRAYER POINTS FOR PROVISION

1. Ask the Lord to provide for the family materially.
   - Pray for Him to literally give you and your family your "daily bread," which includes today your various needs—food, housing, clothes, transportation, and other necessities (Matthew 6:11, NIV).
   - Ask Him to provide the opportunities to work and make money.
   - Thank Him for His provision.

2. Ask God to provide the relationships, opportunities, and environment needed for the health, maturation, and development of the family.
   - Pray for your family to have good, wise, and godly friends.
   - Ask the Lord to open the doors and show you how to prepare to seize opportunities.

3. Pray for family members to learn to walk in wisdom in regard to life, money, and work.
   - Wise people listen to wise instruction.
   - Wise people fear the Lord.
   - Wise people associate with wise people.
   - Wise people preserve what they've gained and use it.
   - Wise people flee from sin.
   - Wise people don't see how close they can get to the precipice without falling off.
   - Wise people plan for the future.
   - Wise people discipline their speech.
   - Wise people are diligent and creative in their work.

- Wise people influence others to trust the Lord.[lix]

4. Ask the Lord to help us know when we need to wait for something and when we need to pursue it.
   - Ask the Lord for the wisdom and patience needed when the right thing to do is to *"wait for the LORD and keep his way"* (Psalm 37:34a, ESV).
   - Pray for wisdom, grit, and courage to get up and take action.

Week One: Known by Name

I love uncovering hidden gems in the Old Testament to apply to our lives today. One set of stones was not quite so obscure. In the book of Exodus, God gave elaborate instructions about the blueprint for the Tabernacle, including the priests' garments. Chapter 28 includes specifics about the breastplate of the high priest.

This breastplate resembled a jeweler's display box, including fine stones like emerald, sapphire, amethyst, and topaz. When Aaron came into God's presence, he literally carried the names of the tribes of Israel on his shoulders and over his heart. What a picture of intercession. He stood before the Lord on behalf of the people, praying for them by name.

As we seek to raise fruit-bearing disciples of Jesus Christ in our homes, I believe Aaron's breastplate offers several valuable lessons.

1. One of the greatest acts of love we can do for our children and grandchildren is to pray for them regularly.

Dr. Jerry Falwell said, "Nothing of eternal significance ever happens apart from prayer."[lx] Through prayer we invite God into their circumstances. We ask Him to supernaturally get involved where we cannot. We admit in prayer, "God, as much as I love my child, You can do so much more for him than I can in this situation."

Sometimes when I experience difficulty as an adult, I lift up a prayer for my children and say, "Lord, when they go through a similar situation in their adult years, please help them." The Lord, who is timeless, is fully able to do just that.

2. We are precious to the Lord.

God wanted the names of His children engraved on very costly stones. Then and now, gems are considered valuable. Aaron's stunning cover of sparkling blue, red, green, and purple stones not only caught the eyes of the Israelites, the precious stones received the Lord's attention. Our children are precious to us, and God's children are none the less to Him. The Lord once reminded the Israelites, *"You are precious in my sight and honored, and I love you"* (Isaiah 43:4a, CSB).

That doesn't mean life will be easy and free of pain. But we can take confidence in the omniscience of God, who knows all things and all people—including our children.

3. God knows us—and our children—by name.

The fine stones alone would have made the breastplate amazing. But that was not enough for the Lord. He wanted the names of Jacob's sons on them. And those names specifically represented many other people under each tribe.

Jesus told His followers, *"Aren't two sparrows sold for a penny? Yet not one of them falls to the ground without your Father's consent. But even the hairs of your head have all been counted. So don't be afraid; you are worth more than many sparrows"* (Matthew 10:29-31, CSB).

Through the years, as I've prayed for my own family, I've taken comfort that the Lord is deeply aware of who we are, where we are, and what we are doing. We may not be rich, famous, or on the cover of Forbes magazine, but we are on God's list. And that is enough.

4. We can practice our own ways of memorializing our family to remind us to pray.

When Aaron wore the ephod, he carried the nation's names over his heart, which reminded him to take them to the Lord. We, too, can creatively find ways reminding us to lift our family members to the Lord. When our children were young, some days I carried a small toy or trinket in my pocket like a Lego mini-figure. When I touched it through the day, it reminded me to pray for my children.

Once, while attending a family conference at Ridgecrest Conference Center, we took five decent-sized stones—one for each of our family—out of one of the babbling brooks. Years later, we still have those smooth stones, polished by the constant flow of mountain water, inconspicuously kept in a corner of our yard. They are simple and subtle reminders of God's faithfulness and of my need to pray for our family.

5. We can pray specifically and un-specifically.

As the high priest interceded for the tribes, his prayers represented some known and other unknown needs. Pastor Mark Batterson writes, "The more faith you have, the more specific your prayers will be … When you spell out your prayers with specificity, it will eventually spell God's glory."[lxi]

We all carry explicit needs and wants to the Lord on behalf of our own. But I'm thankful we can also intercede without knowing exactly what they need. I may simply say, "Lord, you know what my child will experience today, what You desire to accomplish in his life, and how to work what is best for Your purposes. I lift him to You and ask You to meet his needs according to Your riches."

Don't underestimate the value of your prayers in the raising of your children. A prayer you offer today may touch the life of your child moments from now—or decades later—through the powerful throne of grace.

Jesus can take care of our treasures. As parents, we are wise to practice praying for all of our children's lives, quietly entrusting them to His care. And we can entrust those treasures to Him because of our sixth prayer word beginning with the letter **P: Presence.**

One Psalm that speaks much of the presence of God is Psalm 139, one to which we should routinely return for some basic theological reminders. It could be called the *omni* psalm because it deals with God's omniscience, omnipresence, and omnipotence. In verses 7-12, King David wonders at the reality that God is everywhere: *"Where shall I go from your Spirit?*

Or where shall I flee from your presence? … If I say, 'Surely the darkness shall cover me, and the light about me be night,' even the darkness is not dark to you; the night is bright as the day" (vs. 7, 11-12a, ESV).

Amazingly, things that are dark to us are light to God. We may be in the dark, but He's in the bright light. He sees everything, He knows everything, and He is everywhere.

During my senior year of high school, I began the daily discipline of spending time alone with the Lord in prayer and Bible meditation. I moved to Presbyterian College in the fall of that year into Bailey Hall, the dorm for freshmen guys. Over thirty years later, I can vividly remember sitting at my desk on the third floor of Bailey, looking out over the oak tree outside our window, and practicing my daily devotions with the Lord. The realization impacted me, *God is just as much here as He is in Greenville, South Carolina. He is not limited to my parents, our house, or the church I attended. I have just as much access to Him here as I did at home.* That is because of the omnipresence of God.

On Saturdays, I ask God to make His presence known in and through my family. In the same way my family and I need the Lord's presence, Moses needed it as well, faced with the daunting task of leading several million Israelites through the desert. To make matters worse, these fickle people made a golden idol in an idolatrous act against Jehovah. The people were immature, unstable, and often ungodly. Moses knew that apart from the daily, manifest presence of the One who appeared to him at the burning bush, his leadership was doomed. Moses needed God in his life every day. God was going to have to guide him, encourage him, and provide for him.

Personally Going with Us

Moses requested the Lord make Himself real to Moses, and *"The Lord replied, 'My Presence will go with you, and I will give you rest.' Then Moses said to him, 'If your Presence does not go with us, do not send us up from here'"* (Exodus 33:14-15, NIV).

I love how the New Living Translation words verse fourteen: *"The Lord replied, 'I will personally go with you, Moses.'"*

When we pray for the Lord's presence in the lives of our children, we are asking, *God, please manifest Your presence in their lives.* The word *manifest* refers to "God's hand at work in inescapably evidential ways."[lxii]

Through the years, I've respected Pastor Jack Hayford. Though we come from different church traditions, I've appreciated his integrity, heart for worship, and faithfulness to shepherd God's people with God's Word. My wife and I heard him speak several years ago at The Billy Graham Training Center at The Cove in Asheville, North Carolina. I thanked him for his book *Manifest Presence,* which invites believers to expect a visitation of God's grace through worship. He told me that a few years after the release of the book, the publishers decided to change the name to *The Reward of Worship* because so many people didn't understand what *manifest presence* meant.

When we ask God to manifest His presence, we're wanting Him to make Himself real to a person and in a situation. Pastor Hayford writes: "Essentially, it is God's presence— the raw dynamic of His Being and Person stepping into a situation—that gives place to His transforming, redeeming, delivering power." The Lord's dynamic presence includes His objective omnipresence, relating to all humanity, as well as His abiding presence, which is more subjective and personal. Because of both of these realities, believers everywhere can "call upon Him to manifest His presence in their midst or certain situations" as they worship and follow Him.[lxiii]

On Saturdays, I ask the Lord to make His presence known in and through our family.

Questions to Consider

1. How does it affect your attitude toward intercession to know the Lord thinks His children are precious?
2. What simple reminder can you give yourself today to pray for your children?
3. How can you memorialize for your family something the Lord has done?

Prayer for this Week

Father, thank You for personally going with us. How grateful I am that You know each of us by name. As we seek to follow You, I ask You to manifest Yourself in the life of my family. Cause us to know You more and more, experiencing You at work in our lives. Amen.

If you want to skip to week one of Protection, head to page 215.

Week Two: Pouring Forth

What Do We Expect?

The gospel writers Matthew and Mark both record one of the saddest commentaries in all of Scripture. Jesus returns to His hometown, teaches in the synagogue, and performs a few healing miracles. The people are astonished at His wisdom and power. But they are unable to accept the reality right in front of their eyes because it did not fit their preconceptions of Jesus. They knew His family and had witnessed His childhood. They could not welcome Him as more than the carpenter's son. The Bible says, *"And he did not do many mighty works there, because of their unbelief"* (Matthew 13:58, ESV).

In some arenas, God limits the extent of His activity to the faith and expectation of His people. He wants to be believed, trusted, and welcomed to come and do "mighty works." When I pray for the Lord to make His presence known, I am saying, "Lord, I surrender. I need You. I can do nothing apart from

You. Please come, move, glorify Yourself, and make Yourself known so that we and others may love, trust, and believe You."

One patriarch continued expecting from God, even when it seemed impossible. Abraham was ninety-nine years old, and he and Sarah were still childless. Yet twenty-four years earlier God promised them descendants. They knew that within their own physical abilities and reproductive powers, they had no hope. The Bible says: *"Even when there was no reason for hope, Abraham kept hoping—believing that he would become the father of many nations. For God had said to him, 'That's how many descendants you will have!' And Abraham's faith did not weaken, even though, at about 100 years of age, he figured his body was as good as dead—and so was Sarah's womb"* (Romans 4:18-19, NLT).

God stepped in one year before Sarah would give birth to a son and revealed a new, precious name to Abraham: *"The Lord appeared to him and said, 'I am El-Shaddai—God Almighty. Serve me faithfully and live a blameless life. I will make a covenant with you, by which I will guarantee to give you countless descendants'"* (Genesis 17:1-2, NLT).

You probably have friends who are so dear that just seeing a picture of them or hearing their names encourages you. As we learn them and get to know Him better, God's names can be that way to us.

God revealed Himself as El Shaddai. The word *El* means *might or power.* Shaddai literally means *sufficient.*

El Shaddai is our pourer-forth, our sufficiency, our One who satisfies. Imagine a crying baby who can only be satisfied by his mother's milk. Kay Arthur explains, "This is El Shaddai, the pourer-forth, who pours Himself out for His creatures

... and says, "Come unto me and drink" ... "Open wide thy mouth and I will fill it."[lxiv]

Abraham could choose to trust God, in spite of the deadness of their situation, because He knew El Shaddai, the all-sufficient One who could meet every need, even in impossible situations: "Everything you and I will ever need can be found in the all-sufficient One, God Almighty. This is the truth the name El Shaddai proclaims. The truth came home to Abram with his face in the dust before the Almighty." Surely, he remembered the name when he looked into the face of baby Isaac and watched him grow into a young man. Obstacles, difficulties, and need present no problem to El Shaddai.[lxv]

Knowing God as our El Shaddai, the One who is ever-present and always able to meet our needs, gives us courage to keep asking for the needs in our lives and those of our family. Praying for God's presence includes asking the Lord three requests, each one beginning with the letter **P: pour, power, and prosperity.**

Pour

When the disciples followed Jesus, they literally walked with Him. They woke up in the morning, looked at Jesus, and expected Him to lead. In our day, God has left us the Holy Spirit. He comes alongside believers to help, comfort, convict, guide, and most importantly, to manifest the person and presence of Jesus in, through, and around us.

It is only the Christian, filled with and controlled by the Holy Spirit, who can please God. The fleshly, natural, carnal Christian cannot please God. Only the spiritual man, empowered by God's Spirit, can carry out the will of the Father.

One key in genuine revival is believers realizing they are not controlled by the Spirit of God. He is unable to flow through our lives when self is on the throne instead of Jesus. God doesn't fill us when we are already full of ourselves.

The Bible often uses the image of pouring to describe the blessing, anointing, and manifesting of the presence of God. Priests and prophets poured oil onto the head of persons chosen to serve in special offices or functions. Oil had a medicinal and protective use, as mentioned by King David in Psalm 23: *"You anoint my head with oil"* (v. 5b, ESV). In another Psalm, he compared the unity between brothers to *"the precious oil on the head, running down on the beard … running down on the collar of his robes"* (133:2, ESV). It is a picture of God pouring out His blessing on His people.

The Lord never intended for believers to live the Christian life through their own energy. There is only one way to experience the successful life of faith, and that is when the Holy Spirit is fueling us with the life of Jesus. Paul exhorts the Ephesians, *"Be filled with the Holy Spirit"* (5:18b, NLT). The idea is to keep on being filled continuously by the Spirit. The real question is, "Who is providing the gasoline for our lives?"

Evil has existed in every generation. Though modern technology allows it to be broadcast in high definition, people have chosen sin for eons. In every new generation, God wants to release the power of His life-giving Spirit in fresh ways. From the days of Genesis to the twenty-first century, the Spirit of God is essential to godly living. I want the Lord to pour Himself out on my children and descendants. I know the Lord is greater than any wicked influence, scheme, or trap from the enemy, and I want His manifest presence at work in my family.

During my sophomore year of college, Dr. Charles Stanley's book *The Spirit-Filled Life*[lxvi] was released, and he preached a companion sermon series on his radio broadcast. I remember devouring these materials, learning step-by-step what it meant to live under the fullness of the Spirit in moment-by-moment dependence on Him. This life of drawing from the Lord as our Source is what Jesus meant in His teaching about the branches and the vine in John 15.

Dr. Stanley writes:

> As the branch draws its life from the vine, so we draw life from Christ. To abide in Christ is to draw upon His life. ... God never, ever, intended for His children—that includes you—to live a life characterized by defeat ... The Holy Spirit is God's answer to the problem of righteous living. He is the abiding presence of Christ's life in you."[lxvii]

We must learn to abide—or remain—in the Vine in order to stay connected to Him and draw from Him, the Source of our strength. The primary purpose of our spiritual practices like Bible reading or meditation, intercession, worshiping with believers on the Lord's Day, and being quiet before Him is to place ourselves into His presence in order to be renewed, refocused, and refilled with His life. And learning to do this makes all the difference in the world.

As I pray for God to manifest His presence in the lives of my children, I'm asking Him to help them live under the lordship of Jesus Christ, be filled with the Spirit of God, and learn to walk with Him.

Life includes many twists and turns, trials, and at times darkness and troubles. But a life of walking in the Spirit can navigate through such stormy waters. Bill Bright, one of the great statesmen of faith in the twentieth century, wrote: "Walking in the Spirit means walking in faith. ... Keep in step with the Spirit, and you will learn total dependence upon our Great God and Savior."[lxviii]

As we ask God to pour Himself out upon our children and grandchildren, we will then want to boldly ask Him for His power and prosperity. We'll look at those requests in the next chapter.

Questions to Consider

1. What area of your life do you need to ask God to increase your faith, so as not to limit His work by unbelief?
2. Where in your life or family in this season do you need God to be your El Shaddai?
3. Ask the Lord to fill you afresh with His Spirit as you surrender to Jesus Christ.

Prayer for this Week

El Shaddai, You are the Pourer-forth, the All-sufficient One. Take my eyes off of my meager ability and resources and onto Yours. Pour Your Spirit out on me, my children, and my grandchildren, that we may walk in Your blessing, power, and enthusiasm. Amen.

If you want to skip to week two of Protection, head to page 223.

PRAYER FOR PRESENCE

Week Three: Power and Prosperity

When we are praying for the manifest presence of God in our families, we're not just talking about an intellectual knowledge of God that we learn from a sermon or Bible lesson. We're expecting an experiential knowledge—or experience—of the Lord.

In our Western minds, we often think of *knowing* as *assenting to a prescribed set of facts.* However, a biblical concept of knowing is much deeper. The Hebrew word *yada,* translated *to know,* includes the meanings *to perceive and see, to find out and discern, to know by experience, to make known, and to be made known.* Genesis even uses the word to describe lovemaking between spouses.[lxix] To *yada* the Lord is to know Him experientially in the ups and downs of life. It involves taking what we learn in a Bible study, sermon, or devotional time and then walking by faith, trusting the God of the Scriptures to be who He says He is in the realities of our world.

We looked last week at asking God to pour His Spirit out

upon us as we desire His presence in our lives. As we do that, we can also pray for His power and prosperity in the lives of those we love.

Power

In Matthew 13:58, the words "mighty miracles" come from the Greek word *dunamis,* which means *power, ability, or might.* The verse literally means that Jesus did not do powerful deeds in that city. We get our word *dynamite* from *dunamis.* Paul said the gospel *"is the power [dunamis] of God for salvation"* (Romans 1:16, ESV). Later, the apostle revealed God's promise to him in his utter weakness: *"My grace is sufficient for you, for my power is made perfect in weakness"* (2 Corinthians 12:9, ESV).

Life is not easy. Our children's lives will be different than they expected and much harder than you expected when they were young. When newlyweds stand at the altar, they dream of all the good things that will happen. I doubt if many think, *Life will be stressful at times. We will get on each other's nerves. We will have financial struggles. We may lose our jobs. We will watch our parents die. One of us may watch the other one die of cancer. Our children may give us heartache.*

The first time Tracey and I held hands was on a Sunday night at church. At the close of the service, the pastor told us to join hands with the person standing next to us. I rejoiced and thought, *Please pray a long time.* I still remember that evening a young woman sang the solo, "Life is Hard, but God is Good," by Pam Thrum. Well, ain't that the truth?

Tracey and I have journeyed through unexpected trials, heartaches, and valleys. The stress and challenges that come with being a couple in pastoral ministry have at times been daunting and disappointing. Pastoring a church the first year of marriage was what I call *being baptized with fire*. Whatever your lot in life, it will include difficult times.

In such times, we need the Lord's power. And our children will need His power that comes from His presence in their lives. We—and they—can live off of the promise in Deuteronomy 33:25b, *"As your days, so shall your strength be"* (ESV).

Strength to Stand

The night before my grandfather's funeral, I spent the evening with my grandmother, whom I called Mom-ee. Before going to bed, she wanted to tell me about his final moments. Pa-Pa had been very sick for several weeks in a nursing home. Months of taking dialysis had taken its toll on his eighty-two-year-old body.

Mom-ee told me, "Just the other night, I got down on my knees and prayed, 'Lord, please don't let him die alone in the nursing home. Please let me be with him when he dies.'" That Tuesday, Pa-Pa got very sick and was rushed to the hospital. Mom-ee and my aunt stayed in the waiting area while the hospital workers attended him. A doctor came to them and announced, "Mrs. Hendrix, his vital signs are rapidly dropping. You need to come see him right away."

Her legs feeling like lead weights, Mom-ee thought, *There is no way I can go in there and watch my husband die. I can't* do this. But she quietly asked God to help her. She and my aunt walked through the double doors to the bed where Pa-Pa lay. Here was her husband, friend, and lover of more than five decades. For about forty of those years, he preached the gospel as he pastored different churches. When he was a boy, he was so rambunctious—wild as a monkey—that his family gave him the nickname *Monk*. For the rest of his life, many people called him Rev. Hendrix, but his siblings and wife affectionately called him Monk.

On that hospital bed, Pa-Pa couldn't talk and looked weak. My aunt patted his head and kept saying, "Daddy, we love you." The nurse told Mom-ee to start talking to help him die peacefully.

"Monk, I have loved you for more than fifty-eight years. Now you are about to go to heaven. You're going to see Jesus. You've talked about heaven many times. Now you're going, and then I'm coming. So you go on."

Pa-Pa moved his throat as if to say something. He closed his eyes and was immediately in God's presence. Mom-ee told me the story sitting upright on her bed. She relayed the account to me without shedding a tear. Proud of herself for having the strength to stand upright and speak clearly to her husband in his last moments, she knew God was her helper.

When we face challenging moments, God is present with us. Our hurdle may be facing a difficult situation at home, a boss we dislike, or a financial obstacle. The Bible promises God's presence in every situation—even the ones that cause fear or stress. Let's ask Him daily for the strength to face them. And let's ask Him to be the strength our children need in their times of weakness. Then we can move forward, standing in His strength one moment at a time.

Prosperity

Not only do we need the pouring out of God's Spirit on our lives and the power He gives moment by moment, but we ask for His prosperity. Yes, I know the "prosperity gospel" in America has made a mockery of this biblical concept, and unfortunately, numerous television preacher personalities made a fortune promising health and wealth. But remember, the abuse of a truth is not reason enough to throw the truth out altogether. Instead, we should seek to strike a biblical balance.

In John's third epistle, he greets them with this word: *"Brethren, I pray that in all respects you may prosper and be in good health, just as your soul prospers"* (3 John 2, NASB). In essence, the apostle is asking God to bless them in every way, mindful of the truth from Psalm 127 that if the Lord is not building our house, the workers are wasting their time. The word *prosper* comes from the Greek word *euodoo,* which means *to help on one's way or journey.*

John is hoping God will help his readers along their journey of life. Isn't that what we want for our children? It comforts me to know that as my children become young adults and I am not always there to help them, the Lord can help them on their journey. One day, when I am in heaven and no longer here to offer advice, comfort, or encouragement, the Lord can come alongside them and help them on their way. And it actually excites me that God answers my prayers for years after I pray them—and years after I leave this earth. He can keep on helping my descendants.

Ray Edwards wrote an entire helpful book, *Permission to*

Prosper, explaining the word *prosperity* from a biblical perspective and showing how thriving businesses are one of the greatest tools to glorify God and accomplish Jesus' Great Commandment and Great Commission. He details that the word *prosper* appears 48 times in the Bible; *prosperity,* 26; and *prosperous,* eight. He explains, "True, biblical prosperity is about receiving everything that God has in store for us and stewarding it for His glory."[lxx]

Another word for prosperity is simply *blessing.* What does *blessing* mean? In a biblical worldview, I believe praying for a blessing is asking God to cause something to produce more with His hand on it than can be naturally produced without Him.

At the infamous account of the feeding of the five thousand, which was actually five thousand men, not counting women and children, the Bible says they only had five loaves and two fish. But Jesus said, *"Bring them here to Me"* (Matthew 14:18, ESV). Sometimes, that's all it takes. We see our helpless situation, our tiny strength, and our limited resources. And naturally, with human eyes, it seems impossible. But Jesus says, "Bring that situation or person to Me." We may have to bring it to Him once, or we may have to bring it to Him a thousand times, but we keep bringing it to Him.

Then He tells the crowd to sit down. That's humorous to me. If I read between the lines correctly, He is saying, "I don't need your help. Just please sit down and let Me work."

Matthew then records, *"Taking the five loaves and the two fish, He looked up to heaven and said a blessing"* (14:19, ESV).

Jesus blessed the tiny meal. And what happened when the

meal received His blessing? God produced more with His hand on the meal than could be naturally produced without Him. The disciples began passing out the baskets to the crowd, and the bread and fish continuously multiplied so that *"they all ate and were satisfied"* (vs. 20, ESV). What a blessing.

When we pray prosperity over our children, we are saying, *Lord, please get involved in this situation in their lives—health, finances, job, house, relationships, marriage, parenting, emotions, mind, ministry, or influence. Please work in such a way to cause more to be produced supernaturally than can take place in our own energies.*

Questions to Consider

1. What does it mean biblically to "know" God?
2. Where specifically do you need God's power in your life and family?
3. What situation, need, or person do you need to confidently ask God to prosper?

Prayer for this Week

Father, thank You for not leaving us alone but for giving Your presence. I ask for Your power to strengthen me for the needs, tasks, and trials facing me. As I bring my requests to You, I ask for You to prosper my life, causing more to be accomplished supernaturally than naturally possible. Amen.

If you want to skip to week three of Protection, head to page 231.

PRAYER FOR PRESENCE

Week Four: A Multi-Generational Vision

The following was written in 2003 by my friend Gene Brooks, a missionary to Liberia with SIM:

God was at work. Three years ago our pastor asked us to begin to pray for an unreached people group called the Sh'ui people in southwest China. He began to give out fact sheets on the Sh'ui people during our prayer meetings. We could not pronounce any of the words. We had no idea how our denomination's mission board connected us with this hidden people whom nobody, especially we, had ever heard of. But we were willing to pray for them, and we prayed our feeble prayers over the next several months. Some people in the church did not have much of a vision for praying for the Sh'ui people. A few people did.

One of those was Tom. He made a commitment to Christ at a young age, but family, a career in the National Guard, and the cares of the world stifled out that fire that burned for Christ.

Many years later, after raising a family and being successful in the Guard, health problems involving Tom's leg and back forced him into early retirement and disability. During that time of forced stillness, God began to speak to Tom again. He began wrestling with God as Jacob had wrestled with God at Peniel. Just as God injured Jacob in his hip before he let go, Tom was injured in his hip so God could get a hold of him. The next Sunday, Tom came to our church. Right in the middle of communion, as the bread was being passed, Tom started limping down the aisle.

"I can't wait," he said aloud, "I have to repent now." And down the aisle he hobbled, a man come back to God. Pastor Rhett ministered to Tom between communion duties, and the flame of Christ came back into Tom's life as a blaze. A blaze of prayer. God called Tom to the indispensable duty of intercession in the life of our church.

For Tom, the unreached Sh'ui people became his prayer priority. He promoted prayer for them, continually asked for prayer for them during Wednesday night prayer meeting, prayed long hours himself, and made them his project. I was leading the new prayer team at our church at the time, and we put Tom on the team. He was a bulwark, and he made sure we never forgot to pray for the Sh'ui.

About two years ago, Tom told me he was led to pray that *The JESUS Film* would be translated into the Sh'ui language. I told him, "Tom, you can pray for that, but I have seen the websites on this people group. Only the old people and priests among them speak their language now. No one else really does. I think it would be a waste of your prayer time." But Tom was adamant. He knew God had called him to pray for *The JESUS Film* to be recorded in their language, and he prayed for it.

At the beginning of 2002, three years after we began praying for the Sh'ui people, Pastor Rhett was called to another church. We started a neighborhood Lighthouse Bible study which Tom joined, and we committed ourselves to continue praying for the Sh'ui people. By email, I surprisingly connected with some believers who were working among this people who happened to be visiting our state that summer. They came to our Bible Study one night to present what was happening among our adopted people group.

Three and a half to four years ago there were very few Sh'ui believers and no Scripture translated into their language. While historically there had been some Catholic ministry in their area, no known fruit remained.

But three years ago, something changed. The Lord sent missionaries from our church's denomination for the first time to work among the Sh'ui. Other agencies increased activity the same year. Though no one can know any hard numbers among them because of the government situation, they guesstimated that 500 Sh'ui believers exist today.

We realized this was the same time Pastor Rhett led us to begin praying for them. Tom sat there in the Bible Study with his bad leg propped up on an ottoman. If you knew him, you could see he was beginning to get choked up.

One of the big problems is that no Scripture is translated into the heart language of the Sh'ui. While most of the Sh'ui can speak Mandarin, the language they speak at home and from their heart is Sh'ui. Two years ago, God called a man to translate *The JESUS Film* into the Sh'ui mother tongue. As of that night's Bible Study, they were completing the translation with native Sh'ui speakers. Four years ago, this translation would have been impossible because there were no known Sh'ui believers. Now there were enough to do all the male and female parts of the Gospel of Luke on *The JESUS Film*.

Tom's eyes swelled. Tears came down his face. He began to shake. Then he could hold it in no longer. He shouted, "Hallelujah! Thank you, Lord! Never did I ever expect to hear what You were doing among the Sh'ui in answer to our prayers. Tonight You brought to our little Bible Study these people who live with them and love them and know them. You brought them all the way around the world to show us Your work, to show us how You are answering our prayers. O God! Thank You!"

The Scripture says Jacob walked with a limp the rest of his life. Whenever I see Tom walking with his limp, I think of how he wrestled with God, how God touched his life and made him an intercessor for a forgotten people far away.

∽

Leaving a Multi-Generational Legacy

God can use your life to leave a legacy that outlasts you. Your prayers could touch descendants and people you will never meet until heaven.

We live in a day marked by a downward spiral morally and spiritually. It's easy in such times to retreat in spiritual battle rather than "forward march." Parents and grandparents today need a vision for the Lord getting involved in their family line and causing them to prosper spiritually, leaving a rich legacy of godliness for generations to come.

A little-known hero in the Old Testament book of 2 Kings left a legacy that lasted at least two hundred years. Jonadab, in the midst of massive cultural decline, believed the Word of God, embraced holiness, and created standards for his family to help them be faithful to the Lord and be wise in a wicked society.[lxxi] He knew that even in dark times, God could be trusted, and He would not forget those who honored Him. The book of Jeremiah records an incident some two hundred years later that reveals his descendants were still honoring God and still living by the house rules set by their ancestor. His life of devotion to God impacted many generations, and so can ours. We, too, need a multi-generational vision for our lives.

In our day of instant gratification, we can resist cultural norms of only living for today and instead embrace the vision of a godly legacy that outlives us. In their excellent book, *The Promise of Jonadab: Building a Christian Family Legacy in a Time of Cultural Decline,* E. Ray Moore and Gail Pinckney Moore share, "One man's faith in God's Word had spawned at least eight generations of obedience and faithfulness, and his faithful application of that Word provided protection throughout those generations."[lxxii] Jonadab had a vision to not just survive, but thrive, in a way that impacted many lives and bore much godly fruit.

Parents and grandparents, we can plead with God to put His hand upon our families and keep it there long after we leave this earth. Ask Him to prosper your line spiritually. Ask

Him to produce *"oaks of righteousness, the planting of the Lord, that he may be glorified"* (Isaiah 61:3b, ESV) through your lineage. And may He still be bringing Himself glory and producing Jesus-followers through your descendants long after you are gone. That would be the greatest kind of prosperity we can experience.

As we learn to live in light of the presence of God, we realize He has the power to keep us and preserve us in a dangerous world.

Questions to Consider

1. Do you have a multi-generational vision for your life and family?
2. How can you embrace a vision to not just survive, but thrive, in a way that impacts many lives and bears godly fruit?
3. What can you do to make an impact in the present that may keep making a difference long after you are gone?

Prayer for this Week

Father, it's so easy to only have a vision to survive in the present. Help me to embrace a vision that far outlasts my own life. Pour Your Spirit out on my children and grandchildren, and may multiple generations that follow bring honor to Your name. Amen.

If you want to skip to week four of Protection, head to page 239.

PRAYER POINTS FOR PRESENCE

1. Ask the Lord to manifest His presence, making Himself real and known in and through your family.
   - Thank God for His constant omnipresence that spans everywhere.
   - Ask the Lord to enable us to grow in godliness and faith, inviting Him to work in our lives.
   - Pray for God to manifest His abiding presence in the lives of those for whom we pray.

2. Pray for God to abundantly bless to overflowing the life, health, witness, and resources of the family. Ask Him to prosper you in every way in your lives.
   - Bring the various areas of your life to Him, submitting them to Him to work through as He pleases.
   - Ask Him to help you live in such a way that invites blessing.
   - Ask the Lord to bless your family's resources, providing and supplying out of His abundance.

3. Ask Him to sovereignly cause all of you to supernaturally produce more than would be naturally possible.
   - Thank the Lord that He is always ahead of you and is able to weave a thousand myriad strings together to accomplish His purposes.
   - Just as God is able to multiply kingdom influence again and again, ask Him to work through your lives in ways that can only be explained by His blessing.

4. Ask God for an outpouring of His Spirit upon your sons and daughters:
   - Experiencing Him in dynamic ways.
   - Flowing in creativity, enthusiasm, and divine energy.
   - Empowering and enabling them to live abundant lives.

5. Ask God to keep working in your family's line for generations to come.
   - May the blessing that results from your prayers continue for many years and decades. May it outlive you.
   - May the kingdom of God be extended mightily through the blessing of God coming upon those for whom you pray.

PRAYER FOR PROTECTION

Week One: A Seeing God

A Critical Opportunity

As our children become teenagers and young adults, we parents feel our great inability to control their lives. Unlike the preschool years when they were at our feet, now that they are driving cars, working a job, or off at college, we have a limited amount of power to protect, guide, and nurture them.

I've prayed for my children all their lives, but now I see it as a critical opportunity to ask God to stay active in their lives. We can make lists from the Scriptures to pray daily. Because I know my children well, I can ask God about specific things related to each one. I've recently found help by using some books that include recorded prayers for your family, like *When You Don't Know What to Pray* by Charles Stanley, *The Power of Praying for Your Adult Children Book of Prayers* by Stormie Omartian, and *Praying the Scriptures for Your Adult Children: Trusting God with the Ones You Love* by Jodie Berndt.

We can even pray for children or grandchildren who are not yet conceived. What a privilege to invite the Lord to be at work in their lives in the future. And we ask the Lord to help us walk in His ways and make good decisions now that will be a help to them tomorrow.

Taking a Risk

For weeks my daughter tried unsuccessfully to ride her bicycle without training wheels. Fearing falling, she would not peddle forward and stay on the bike. We lived in the country. A large rolling hill faced the front of the house. Anna-Frances and I sat down in the white rocking chairs on the porch, facing the hill.

Slowly moving back and forth next to my six-year-old, I asked, "Do you remember the Bible story about Peter walking on the water? In a great storm, the disciples experienced fear. When Jesus came walking on the water, they were afraid. They had never seen anyone do that before. What did Peter do that no one else did?"

"He got out of the boat and walked on water."

"That's right, honey," I replied. "He tried something new and trusted God to care for him even though it was scary."

She quietly and thoughtfully listened, so I asked, "Anna, what do you think God wants you to do with this bike?"

"Trust Him and try to ride."

We arose and walked the bicycle to the very top of the large green hill. She mounted, and I held on from behind. As she began peddling, I ran behind her. Knowing she had her balance, I let go of the bike and yelled, "Go, Anna! You've got it, babe!"

Watching her peddle that bike all the way to the hill's bottom remains one of my favorite memories from that season of our lives. She got out of the boat and rode without training wheels.

Episodes of Letting Go

Parenting involves numerous episodes of learning to let go. At the toddler stage, we let go of their hands as they learn to waddle a few steps on their own. We give up more control when they spend the night for the first time with grandparents.

Taking them to Sunday school, small groups, or Bible study at church includes releasing them temporarily into the care of a group of teachers and volunteers. Sending them to summer camp, leaving them with babysitters, and entrusting them to teachers and tutors for their schooling all involve some level of risk and conferring authority to someone other than yourself.

When Anna-Frances was four, her mother served as our church's minister of music, which meant she was out the door early on Sunday morning, leaving Dad to get three preschoolers ready for church. I never got the knack of fixing a little girl's hair, so I learned to show up at her four-year-old classroom holding her hair bow and hairbrush. Her teacher was always glad to help me out and fix her hair. That was one release I was glad to do. And it made my little girl look a lot better than if I had tried being her hairdresser.

Other transitions in life don't come so easily. Last year, my little girl turned nineteen, graduated from high school, and began her college career. She doesn't need any help fixing her hair now and knows how to do a whole lot of other things by herself too. How quickly the years flew from this vantage point. It seems I was just taking her to the preschool hall at church in her pastel smock dresses. Yet Daddy and Mommy had to calm our hearts, wipe our tears, and trust that we had raised a responsible young adult.

The Bible is full of instructions about learning to release those things dear to us.

- King David exhorted, *"Cast your burden on the Lord, and he will sustain you"* (Psalm 55:22, ESV).

- The Lord Jesus challenged us to release generously that to which we cling, *"Give, and it will be given to you … For with the measure you use, it will be measured to you"* (Luke 6:38, NIV).

- The apostle Peter encouraged, *"Give all your worries and cares to God, for he cares about you"* (1 Peter 5:7, NLT). The idea in the Greek text is like a man with a heavy backpack taking off the load and leaving it at God's feet.

Elisabeth Elliot spoke in several of her books about how God gives us material for sacrifice—longings, hopes, and joys of the soul that He requires us to give back to Him. She wrote:

> "The very longings themselves can be offered to Him who understands perfectly. The transformation into something He can use for the good of others takes place only when the offering is put into his hands."[lxxiii]

We all long for God to protect our children. And all fear the horrific news some parents endure when a child has been seriously injured or killed. What parent's heart does not flutter a little when they see their child drive off in a car or take off in an airplane?

The God Who Sees

The book of Genesis records the account of Hagar, an Egyptian maidservant of Abram's wife Sarai (later called Sarah). If you know their story, you know that although God promised Abram offspring, in their old age Sarai still had not yet born a child. She looked around and reasoned with her natural sight, and she concocted a plan: Abram could sleep with Hagar and get her pregnant. Sarai thought, *"Perhaps I can build a family through her"* (Genesis 16:2b, NIV). Yes, I know that sounds way-out-there to our modern thinking, but in that day and culture, it was not uncommon for a man to have sexual relations with maidservants in his keeping.

Sarai did a dangerous thing. She reasoned and planned without God. And Abram also did a dangerous thing. He went along with the plan. He refused to take the high road. There are two things that never go well: making plans without the Lord and having sex with someone other than your spouse. This couple decided to play with fire, and it ended up burning them. And when we play with fire, we don't just burn ourselves, but we scorch others.

Hagar conceived, and jealousy immediately arose in Sarai. She accused her maid of getting uppity and despised her. Again, Abram defers to his wife in an act of cowardice. The Bible says, *"Then Sarai mistreated Hagar; so she fled from her"* (Genesis 16:6, NIV). Today, Hagar could be a poster child for the #MeToo movement, but in her day, she was alone and helpless, so she ran for safety into the desert. Distraught and dejected, she needed a refuge and took comfort by a spring of water.

Then, purposefully and compassionately, the angel of the Lord found her by that spring. Bible scholars believe when the Old Testament refers to "the angel of the Lord," it is actually a pre-New Testament appearance of the second Person of the Trinity. We call that a *theophany,* a "direct, visual manifestation of the presence of God."[lxxiv] God knows exactly where Hagar is, what she is feeling, and what she needs. He speaks a promise to her about her baby's future and even assures her, *"the Lord has heard of your misery"* (Genesis 16:11b, NIV).

At times in my life when I have been stressed out, overwhelmed with problems, or hurt from the actions and attitudes of others, I have run to the Lord and asked Him for help. It may be lying flat on the floor of my study with an open Bible, looking out the window in my car, or in the midst of the hustle and bustle of life. There have been times when God did intervene and act. But more often, instead of a fabulous deliverance, the Lord has a way of simply revealing Himself. It may be through a quiet moment, a song on the radio, an email from a friend, or a Bible verse heard in a sermon. The devotional writer Oswald Chambers once shared he experienced a deep manifestation of the Lord's presence in his life as he simply looked into the face of his pet collie, Tweed.[lxxv] God's assurances can come in a thousand different ways. And in those times, though He doesn't necessarily change the situation, it's as if He says, "I am aware of you and your situation." And in those times, the knowledge of His presence is enough.

After the theophany by the desert spring, Hagar speaks a name of God, the first appearance of it in the Bible: *"You are the God who sees me … I have now seen the One who sees me"* (Genesis 16:13b, NIV). The Hebrew name is El Roi, and it means "The God who sees."

We pray for protection for our family, confident that God sees each one of us. He knows what we are going through. He cares. He is intimately acquainted with all our ways (Psalm 139:3, NASB). El Roi sees your daughter as she drives home from college. He sees your son when he is treated unfairly by a coach or boss. He knows all the ins and outs of a potential new job for you or your spouse. He sees. He knows. He understands. Wayne Grudem writes, "God does not need us for anything; yet it is the amazing fact of our existence that he chooses to delight in us. … This is the basis for personal significance in the lives of all God's people: to be significant to God is to be significant in the most ultimate sense."[lxxvi]

Questions to Consider

1. Have you considered praying for children and grandchildren who have not yet been born?
2. What material for sacrifice do you need to offer to the Lord?
3. How does it affect your praying, understanding that God is El Roi, the God who sees?

Prayer for this Week

Father, it is our very nature as parents to want to control, shelter, and protect our children. But as they grow, I know that I have to release their lives to You step by step. Thank You that You see them when I don't, and I can trust them to Your care. Amen.

Week two for Peace starts on page 39.

PRAYER FOR PROTECTION

Week Two: God Will Take Care of You

Positioning as a Watchman

Ancient cities needed strong, fortified walls for protection. On those walls, kings positioned watchmen to stand guard. The Hebrew word for *watchman* includes "to keep, guard, observe, watch, wait, and pay attention." It contains the idea of protecting and preserving. The prophet Isaiah spoke of this role in Isaiah 62:6-7, taking the picture of a literal watchman from his society and turning it into a symbol potent with spiritual imagery. In these two verses, we see that watchmen do not keep silent. They cling to God's promises and get involved in the lives under their watch.

God sets His people as the spiritual watchmen on the walls in our societies. And He positions parents and grandparents as watchmen over our families. Examples of spiritual watchmen abound in the Scriptures.

Genesis 18 records a divine encounter Abraham experienced with the Lord, where we believe the three members of the Trinity actually came and visited with the patriarch in bodily form. He walked with them, and they revealed their plans to him. The sins of the cities of Sodom and Gomorrah grieved the Lord, and He planned to destroy them for their wickedness. Deeply concerned, as Abraham's nephew lived in Sodom, the Bible gives an incredible snapshot of the habit of a spiritual watchman: *"Abraham remained standing before the Lord"* (Genesis 18:22b, NIV). He then intercedes with the Lord on behalf of these cities, asking the Lord if He finds fifty righteous people there if He will spare the city. The Lord agrees. In typical ancient, Middle Eastern fashion, Abraham continues to barter, asking the Lord to agree to fewer and fewer numbers. Finally, the Lord answers, *"For the sake of ten, I will not destroy it"* (vs. 32b).

I wonder if we grasp that the prayers of righteous people can alter the fate of nations and families. Our children and our descendants need faithful parents and grandparents, aunts and uncles, who stand before the Lord on their behalf.

The prophet Amos saw several visions of judgment coming upon the northern kingdom of Israel. First he saw locusts stripping the land clean of its harvest. Amos stood before the Lord, crying out, "Sovereign Lord, forgive!" And "the Lord relented" (Amos 7:2-3, NIV).

Then he saw fire coming to devour the land, and he cried out, "Sovereign Lord, I beg you, stop!" And "the Lord relented." God even replied, "This will not happen either" (7:5-6)

As evidenced by the prophet's prayers, watchmen understand

the role of the sovereignty and the providence of God in their intercession. And they realize the necessity of the Word of God, praying for God's Word to be honored, remembered, and followed in the lives for whom they pray.

The New Testament includes the essence of the ministry of watchmen. Warning his followers about getting sidetracked by life's anxieties and temptations, Jesus said, *"Keep on the alert at all times, praying that you may have strength"* (Luke 21:36a, NASB). In the Garden of Gethsemane, just an hour before He would be arrested and the disciples would scatter in fear and faithlessness, Jesus asked them to be watchmen in Matthew 26:41.

Most likely, no one will pray for your children and grand-children any more than you. Will you be a watchman over them? James Dobson received the following warning from his father, James Dobson, Sr., in a letter written to him in 1969:

> The greatest delusion is to suppose that our children will be devout Christians simply because their parents have been, or that any of them will enter into the Christian faith in any other way than through their parents' deep travail of prayer and faith.

God Will Take Care of You

In 1947, Frances Hendrix believed the Lord wanted to use her in church-related ministry. She had no idea the many places she would go. God had big plans for this young woman from South Georgia.

The fifth of seven children, she grew up during the Great

Depression. She remembers her family as a place of love and laughter. She shared, "My parents instilled a love for the Bible, the church, and God in me. Honesty, integrity, faith and love were taught by example as well as word. Our home was filled with music which made it easy to memorize a lot of hymns." She remembered walking to school on dirt roads and through cow pastures holding hands with her cousin Verna while singing "God Will Take Care of You."

Her sister Edna came home from a revival meeting one night and asked her younger sister if she had ever considered giving her heart to Jesus. Nine-year-old Frances said yes, and together they knelt by the bedside where she opened her heart to Christ. Soon after she was baptized at Calvary Baptist Church. Frances said, "I have never doubted that I was saved at that time and have never regretted that important decision. God implanted in my heart a deep desire to serve Him."

After graduating in 1939 from Bessie Tift College, a Georgia Baptist School, Frances taught junior high school for nine years. Her life verse became Matthew 6:33, and she chose to believe that as she followed God's call, He would indeed take care of her. She began seminary in Louisville, Kentucky, in 1947. Two years later, after graduating from the school, she received a call that would change her life. Dr. Homer Lindsay, Sr., pastor of First Baptist Jacksonville, Florida, asked Frances to come and serve as the director of youth for their downtown church. She joined the staff in September of 1949, having no idea that she would work there until she retired thirty-five years later.

Frances was the first of three single women Dr. Lindsay,

Sr. would hire. Later would come Guinell Freeman and Fran Hawk. For more than three decades these three women worked together behind the scenes as the church experienced incredible growth, becoming one of the nation's largest churches. At the funeral of Frances Hendrix on January 6, 2014, Dr. Bill Yeldell shared, "These three ladies were the unsung heroes of First Baptist. They were the juice behind the pulpit."

After several years, Frances Hendrix eventually became the director of the church Training Union program for Sunday nights. At the time, First Baptist had the largest standard Training Union in the Southern Baptist Convention. During these years the church experienced tremendous growth, becoming one of the leaders in the nation for outreach, Sunday school, and pulpit ministry. Thousands of people came to know the Lord Jesus Christ. First Baptist Jacksonville became known as "the miracle of downtown Jacksonville."

Frances retired in 1984 but continued teaching a women's Sunday School class for many years. Her extended family tried to convince her to move closer to them in her senior years, but she refused because she would not leave First Baptist Jacksonville.

On January 2, 2014, Frances breathed her last on this earth. The little girl from Georgia who had trusted God to care for her entered her final rest. Many old-time church members, including Fran Hawk, said goodbye to her at a funeral at First Baptist Church Jacksonville on January 6. The next day her body was returned to Columbus, Georgia, for burial next to her parents, and her tombstone includes the inscription of her life verse: *But seek first the kingdom of God and His righteousness, and all these things shall be added to you*" (Matthew 6:33, NKJV).

Frances's grave plot is adjacent to that of her cousin Verna, the one with whom she would hold hands and sing "God Will Take Care of You."

> Be not dismayed whate'er betide,
> God will take care of you;
> Beneath his wings of love abide,
> God will take care of you.
>
> Refrain:
> God will take care of you,
> through ev'ry day, o'er all the way;
> He will take care of you,
> God will take care of you.
>
> Through days of toil when heart doth fail,
> God will take care of you;
> When dangers fierce your path assail,
> God will take care of you.

Another person of a previous generation took great comfort in the words of that hymn. James Cash Penny lost 40 million dollars in the 1929 stock market crash, leaving him with a mountain of debt and false legal accusations made against him. After trying unsuccessfully for two years to overcome his problems, nothing he tried worked, and he had what today we call a nervous breakdown. At age fifty-six, one day while lying in bed in Michigan's Battle Creek Sanitarium, he heard someone singing the hymn, "God Will Take Care of You."

God used that song to speak to James, who surrendered his life at that moment to Jesus Christ, choosing to trust Him for his future. Not only did "he survive his overwhelming difficulties, but he also lived to be ninety-five, built a tremendous financial empire though his JCPenney stores, and was a great philanthropist who helped countless people."[lxxvii]

You see, the Lord's protection is not just about His not letting bad things touch us. It's also about His keeping and preserving us through life so that He maximizes our God-given potential and fulfills His designs for our lives.

Questions to Consider

1. Have you taken your role as a watchman over your family seriously?
2. Where in life do you need the reminder that God will take care of you?
3. How do Frances Hendrix's and J.C. Penny's stories encourage you to keep trusting the Lord?

Prayer for this Week

Father, help me assume my responsibility as a spiritual watchman in my family, church, community, and nation. Thank You that I can trust You at every turn and rest in Your care. Amen.

Week three for Peace starts on page 47.

PRAYER FOR PROTECTION

Week Three: A Firm Foundation

We all want God to protect our families, so on Sundays, I ask the Lord to do just that.

Harold and Betty Killian served numerous churches in the Southeastern United States. I met them when Harold became the Minister of Senior Adults at my home church in Grenville, South Carolina, in the late 1980s. My mother edited Betty's book, *Miraculous Moments,* a personal collection of testimonies of the Lord's faithfulness in their lives. The following account is one of those stories, which Betty gave me permission to share:

During the summer of 1962, my husband was attending Union Theological Seminary in New York City for two weeks of refresher study. It was scheduled before he left that the four children and I would drive from Brevard, North Carolina, to Statesville and Winston Salem in the same state for visits with our families.

The night before they left, Harold awoke from a terrible

dream about two o'clock in the morning. He saw their station wagon suddenly bursting into flames with his wife and children inside. He got up and began praying, pondering whether or not to call Betty in the morning and tell her not to go. He stayed awake for several hours, seeking the Lord.

In the morning, he decided to not call, and his wife and children began their journey. Backing out of their garage, she remembered they had not prayed. She stopped the car in the driveway, and they bowed their heads and asked God to bless them with His protection and give them a happy time together.

They drove about one hundred miles without any problems. As they stopped for a traffic light near Hickory, North Carolina, no cars were in front of them. When the light turned green and Betty accelerated the car, she felt a thump and suddenly the pedal stuck to the floor of the vehicle. With breakneck speed, the wagon lunged forward, smoking and shaking. Betty says, "My hands were glued to the steering wheel from the violent vibrations. I yelled, 'Pull it out,' thinking the accelerator could be manually manipulated. Above the noise, which was similar to a jet plane taking off, the children thought I said, 'Jump out!' Praise God, they didn't attempt that."

Nearing traffic, she began to veer slightly off the road when she spotted a gas station with large gasoline tanks in front of her. She saw a slim possibility of steering between those tanks and the cars to her left. She cried out, "'God, help us.'

He did just that, because a few yards before we would have crashed into the gas tanks, the motor just stopped. We sat there in a smoke-filled car as people rushed to help us."

Betty remembers that amidst all of the stress, she never thought about trying to turn off the ignition. She didn't remove her hands from the violently vibrating steering wheel during the incident for fear that the wagon might turn over or crash into something. She testifies, "I live today along with three wonderful daughters and an equally gifted son because of a miraculous intervention when the motor support broke on our station wagon. He loved us enough to call my husband to pray."

A Firm Foundation

Good parents instinctively want to take care of our children. I remember holding my daughter, Anna-Frances, as a baby in her pink and green nursery many evenings. As she rested in my arms, I would often think how much I wanted to look after, safeguard, and support her. As children of God, we too, look to our heavenly Father for His care and covering of our lives.

One of my all-time favorite hymns, "How Firm a Foundation," originally appeared in John Rippin's 1787 hymnbook. I memorized those lyrics as a college student and have sung them for thirty years. The colorful words embody some powerful promises from God's Word.

How firm a foundation, you saints of the Lord,
is laid for your faith in His excellent Word!
What more can He say than to you He has said,

to you who for refuge to Jesus have fled?[lxxviii]

Believers for more than 230 years have found strength and encouragement from these words about God's presence and protection. Just as I wanted to take care of my baby girl, I also realize as she becomes a young adult, I cannot control her environment and cocoon her like I once could. So I turn to the Lord, who promises to be *"my rock, my fortress and my deliverer"* (Psalm 18:2a, NIV).

When we pray for God to take care of our families, we are wise to remember three words: safety, fingerprints, and sovereignty.

Praying for Safety

Because of His omniscience, omnipresence, and omnipotence, we want God to take care of our families. We live in a world with all sorts of troubles, and we can concur with the line from John Newton's hymn, "Through many dangers, toils, and snares, I have already come; 'tis grace hath brought me safe thus far and grace will lead me home."[lxxix]

The psalmists often prayed for God's safekeeping in verses such as Psalm 5:11, Psalm 20:1, Psalm 34:19, Psalm 46:1, and Psalm 57:1.

For almost four decades, my family has enjoyed many vacations in Daytona Beach, Florida. Often, the trip would include a visit with my great-aunts Frances and Emily, whom I previously mentioned. One year when I was in college, my mother and I made the trip together and met them at a restaurant right off of I-95 in Jacksonville, some 380 miles from our hometown of Greenville, South Carolina. When we left the restaurant, a man approached the four of us, saying his minivan broke down a couple of miles down the road, and he had walked here to call for help (several years before cell phones). His wife remained at the van, and he needed a ride to his vehicle.

You likely have experienced a similar scenario. The Good Samaritan part of you wants to help a stranger in need, but the don't-do-anything-stupid part of you wants some proof that this guy is telling the truth. Not knowing what to do, the four of us asked a few questions and hem-hawed a bit.

I quietly asked the Lord to give us wisdom. It was one of those quick, I-need-help-on-the-spot prayers, like Nehemiah prayed when the king asked, "What is it you want?" The Bible says, *"Then I prayed to the God of heaven, and I answered the king"* (Nehemiah 2:4-5a, NIV).

We had not disclosed where we were from, nor had he. Suddenly, I asked, "So where are you from?"

Out of his mouth came, "Greenville, South Carolina."

I replied, "Oh, wow. We are from Greenville and just drove down here today."

At that moment, I expect he knew his charade was over. So I proceeded to test him, asking a few questions specific to Greenville that any native would know. He could not positively answer any of them, and he failed my test. We told him we could not help him, and the four members of my family said our goodbyes and got into our two vehicles. Two miles down the road, at the spot where he said they were stranded, no van existed.

Only God knows what that man would have done had we

invited him into one of our cars. I expect when he saw my two senior great-aunts, he thought he had found easy targets.

Through the years, I've remembered that moment with amazement. When asked where he was from, he could have said numerous options: Columbus, Ohio; Atlanta, Georgia; Tuscaloosa, Alabama; or a thousand more. But out of his mouth came the one city where we lived, almost four hundred miles away: Greenville, South Carolina. To this day, I believe the Lord was protecting us from harm by putting the name of that specific city in his mouth that summer evening.

The Bible is also replete with examples of the Lord using angels to protect and aid His people. A biblical understanding of reality includes the presence of divine angels in doing God's bidding. Don't underestimate the power of those guardian angels you pray for to cover your children and grandchildren. Oh, the stories that may be told in heaven from dangers we avoided here due to the intervention of the heavenly host.[lxxx]

As an infant, I would not sleep through the night. I cried and cried at night when my parents put me in my crib. They took turns rocking and holding me, helping me fall asleep. Then, when they laid me down in the crib and walked out of the room, I would start wailing again. After several weeks, the routine was wearing on them both. My mother was up with me late one night in our house in Henderson, North Carolina. In faith, she bowed her head and prayed, "Lord, you know Dag and I need to sleep in order to work and take care of this baby. I know You can do all things. Will you send one of your angels here to put Rhett to sleep and help him sleep through the night?"

Ma-Ma, who is not given to theatrics or exaggeration, later shared, "At that moment, I could feel another presence move into the room. Rhett went right to sleep, slept through that entire night, and he never had trouble sleeping again."

The last word I pray for my children each week is for protection. Today we talked about safety. Next week we'll look at God's fingerprints and sovereignty.

Questions to Consider

1. How does Betty's story remind you of the importance of praying parents?
2. Why not write down several Scriptures from this chapter to begin memorizing and praying?
3. What area of life do you need to ask for God's protection?

Prayer for this Week

Father, thank You for giving me a firm foundation in You. Nothing and no one are out of Your reach. I ask You to protect my family from harm, evil, and bad people who would harm them. We run to You. Amen.

Week four for Peace starts on page 55.

Week Four: Fingerprints and Sovereignty

Looking for Divine Fingerprints

We want God to keep us safe. But life happens, problems occur, and dangers come. When they do, we need to look for His divine fingerprints as we peep out the windows.

A hard jump on a mountain bike one evening recently catapulted my teenage son over his handlebars and onto a hard, cement sidewalk, breaking his arm in two places. With one bone piercing through the skin, we hurried to the emergency room, resulting in necessary surgery the next morning. The doctor implanted two metal plates and several screws to correct the fractures.

After the stress of those days, my wife and I took inventory of the evidences of God's goodness and providence in the ordeal. When he crashed, his phone slid out of his pocket up the sidewalk to within arm's reach, so he could immediately call us. We found him facedown on the concrete, unable to move. Had the phone not been reachable, he may have lain there a long time that dark evening. In the ER, the physician's assistant told us, "The doctor on call happens to be an orthopedic surgeon, which makes it the best possible scenario for you all." That surgeon performed the operation the next morning. We also noted our son could have seriously injured himself at that momentum, had he knocked his head on something. Thankfully, only a broken arm occurred. The event afforded the opportunity for an outpouring of love, concern, and prayers from countless friends and family members.

Gratitude for life's enjoyable moments comes easy. But a thankful person trains himself to look for God's graces even in the midst of life's humdrum. We can find everyday provisions of His goodness and grace if we look closely.

Trusting His Sovereignty

It's easy to trust God when He keeps us from harm and grants our comforts. It's hard to trust Him when life hurts.

"Why won't this baby come out?" I grimaced.

On Tuesday, November 7, 2000, my wife checked into Mary Black Hospital in Spartanburg, South Carolina. Due to our unborn baby's size, the doctor induced Tracey early that morning. All day long, parents, sisters, and my grandmother visited and waited for our firstborn baby. We told old family stories, laughed, and sat around my wife's hospital bed. About nine o'clock that night, the dilation was sufficient to begin labor, and Dr. Ketchen wanted Tracey to push.

Thus began two intense hours. For one hundred and twenty

minutes, I stood by the bed as Tracey strained and pushed. Never had I seen her work like she did in that labor. She pushed hard to no avail for three minutes and rested for two. Then Dr. Ketchen instructed, "Do it again." This pattern continued.

After one hour, I grew concerned. I thought, *I know Tracey is doing everything she can. I have never seen her exert herself like this. She can't keep this up for long.*

During the second hour, the baby's head crowned, revealing a spot of black hair, but the head would not come out. I began making trips to the single-person bathroom directly across the hall. Three or four times that hour, I left our room and headed out. Locking the door behind me and kneeling on the hard, cold, tile floor, I cried out to God, "Lord, please make that baby come. You can do anything. Please make his head come out quickly."

Back in the delivery room, the nurses, the doctor, my mother-in-law, and I watched my wife and eyed the tip of the baby's head. He was not moving.

After two hours, I knew my exhausted wife was at her limit. Dr. Ketchen finally asked, "Do you want me to do a C-section?" During the pregnancy, Tracey and I agreed that we wanted a caesarean section to be our last option. Several people told us the difficulties some women have getting over that procedure, and we did not want my wife's twenty-something body to be cut open unless necessary.

"Yes!" my wife exclaimed. "Yes, please do a C-section!"

I quickly agreed, relieved she would not have to endure the agony of labor any longer. The delivery room workers swiftly shifted to plan B. They escorted me out to put on scrubs. "I will see you soon," I told Tracey.

Fifteen minutes later, we met in the cold operating room. I sat at my wife's head and heard the buzz of the saw as they began working. Within moments, we heard the first cry of our baby. Dr. Ketchen lifted him up, and the mother instinct in Tracey immediately raised her arms to try and hold him. After nine months of waiting, Rhett Hendrix Wilson, Jr. was alive and well.

The nurse cleaned up our boy and plopped him into my arms. I proudly looked for the first time into the face of all nine pounds and eleven ounces of my son. They allowed me to carry Hendrix down the hall to the nursery. Walking through the double doors from the OR, I met our four waiting parents. I still have a picture of the five of us enjoying that moment, tears streaming down my face.

Later that night, when my exhausted wife fell asleep, I put my face in my hands and prayed, "Lord, what just happened? Why did that delivery have to be so difficult?"

Several weeks later, my wife went to her six-week checkup. During that time, Tracey shared with Dr. Ketchen, "I really did not want to have to have a C-section." The doctor wisely replied, "You thank God for that caesarean. Hendrix's shoulders were too big to come out of your birth canal naturally. If his head had emerged, there would have been no safe way for me to get him out. Tracey, it would have been fatal for either you or the baby."

How thankful I am we did not have to face that choice. Sometimes God's plan involves waiting, even when we desperately want action now. My cries to God from the bathroom floor did not fall on deaf ears. The Lord knew that quicker is not always better. He had a wiser plan to bless our family.

One difficult but authentic part of our discipleship is accepting the reality that everything in life doesn't work out like we wish. People get cancer and die. Children are killed in car accidents. Spouses check out and leave their families. We lose our jobs, a friend walks away, or our parents get dementia.

As I mentioned earlier, God's protecting power is not just about keeping us satisfied with our creature comforts. It goes much further than that, spanning all of time. From before the creation of the world, the Lord knew who His children would be. He purposed even then that we would bring Him glory. And He wove a tapestry too great for our shortsighted eyes to comprehend. His handiwork includes causing everything that comes into our lives to ultimately be used to bring Him glory and maximize our God-given potential as we trust Him.

Avery Willis and Henry Blackaby wrote:

> "When you have troubles, recognize that God is shaping you and molding you for His purpose. At one time a dazzling diamond was merely a piece of black coal. With pressure, time, and cutting, it became a beautiful jewel!"[lxxxi]

When a small opening appears in a cocoon, the butterfly is not yet ready to emerge. It struggles and struggles for hours to push its body through the hole. During that process of exertion, the wings strengthen and grow, enabling the insect to fly the rest of its life. Without the struggle, the butterfly would never fly.

Even when we fail, God is not thwarted. He uses life's adversities, even our sins and mistakes, to grow us into the persons He wants us to become.[lxxxii]

In life's painful moments, like the butterfly breaking out of its cocoon, we can grow and mature through the hurt.

God had a master plan to take Old Testament Joseph from his native land to Egypt to one day be her Prime Minister. A massive famine would come across the Middle East, and God strategically positioned Joseph to be the brains to literally help save his world. Now, God could have allowed him to remain at home and live a comfortable life. But instead, the Lord protected His plan for Joseph and the world of his day. He allowed him to go through awful deception, betrayal, and pain for years, ultimately leading him out of the prison and into the palace.

As we pray for protection for our families, we can trust His sovereignty. In that word, we see the word *reign*. God reigns over the good and bad, the sunshine and rain, life and death, heaven and hell. Kay Arthur says: "The unshakable fact of God's sovereign control over all is the foundation of sanity in this crazy world. It is the truth that gives stability and order and ultimate hope in this midst of maddening circumstances." The greater we get to know the Lord through His Word and our experiences, the more we realize we can submit to the sovereignty of the Most High, which is all-embracing. We can rest in the reality that "nothing in the universe can touch your life except by His permission and filtered through His fingers of love."[lxxxiii]

An oft-quoted Bible verse is Romans 8:28: *"And we know*

that God causes all things to work together for good to those who love God, to those who are called according to His purpose" (NASB). However, "for good" does not just mean to help you be wealthy, healthy, and happy. Paul explains the "good" in verse 29a: *"For those whom He foreknew, He also predestined to become conformed to the image of His Son"* (NASB). I love how the New Living Translation puts it: *"God knew his people in advance, and He chose them to become like His Son."*

So ultimately, that protecting, keeping, preserving power of God is able to use everything in our lives—past, present, and future—to conform us to the image of Jesus, bring God glory, and maximize the potential He gave us.

I'm so thankful to be held in His hands.

Questions to Consider

1. Where have you seen divine fingerprints even in difficult circumstances?

2. What area(s) of your life and family do you have to trust His sovereignty even when you don't understand His plan?

3. How can you remind yourself that God can work through every aspect of life to bring Himself glory and maximize your potential?

Prayer for this Week

Father, I rejoice in Your sovereignty. Thank you that even in difficult places, I am not forsaken. Help me to release my life to You and trust You to protect and preserve me and my family for Your purposes in this world. Amen.

PRAYER POINTS FOR PROTECTION

1. Pray for safety for your family members and for angels to guard them in all their ways.

2. Ask God to be our protector from Satan and evil, as well as from physical, mental, emotional, or other harm.

3. Ask the Lord for grace to adjust to life's changes and for the enablement to keep moving forward when we hit life's disappointments.

4. Thank God for holding us in His hands.

5. Choose to honor God by trusting Him.

CONCLUSION

The Bible repeatedly warns us not to adopt all of the culture's values as our own. Living a godly and productive life requires swimming upstream. Paul told us in Romans 12, *"Do not be conformed to this world"* (vs. 2a, ESV).

At times we all wonder if any sacrifice is worth it. We see an easier path that many walk and ask ourselves why we put forth all this effort. Parents can daily make choices to be intentional in nurturing and shaping our children. In a world living life upside down, it's easier to just go with the flow and let our kids be sucked into the cesspool of the culture's current. As I said in the first chapter, we have to discipline ourselves so as not to have unguarded homes and ungated lives.

For our children's educational choices, we homeschooled most of their years, allowing us to connect with like-minded families in providing our children a God-centered worldview rooted in the classical model of learning. The majority of that time, we lived off of a pastor's salary of medium to small-size churches. From a monetary and time standpoint, it was a regular sacrifice. But from this vantage point, it was so worth it all.

When I laid in my Bailey dorm room bed as a freshman in 1991, I remember being compelled to start praying for my future children. For years I had already been asking God to provide the suitable wife for me, ever since I heard my boyhood pastor challenge us to do so. But as a college student I asked God to bless my children.

I recall the feeling of helplessness but also of tremendous opportunity when Tracey found out she was pregnant with our first child. Asking the Lord to enable us to be good, wise. and godly parents continued through every stage of the journey—and goes on today. Currently, we have three children in college. And we keep learning that every new season presents unique challenges and obstacles to navigate, needs and opportunities for which to trust God, joys and longings, and adjustments to be made. We never outgrow needing the Lord's help and crying out for His peace, purposes, plans, purity, provision, presence, and protection.

Through the years, we chose to make being together a priority. The gospel of Mark records a simple disciple-making, mentoring principle when Jesus picked His disciples: *"He appointed twelve, that they might be with Him"* (Mark 3:14a, NKJV). We call this the "with Him" principle. Many of life's valuable lessons are caught and not taught, gleaned in the rhythms and routines of much time spent in each other's presence. As our kids become young adults, it's rewarding to realize how much they enjoy home, family, and time together.

A couple of years ago at Christmas, my oldest son gave individual cards to me and my wife. He picked out a thoughtful one, but what he wrote brought the greatest blessing:

Dear Dad, Thanks for being my closest friend and someone that I can trust and depend on. Thanks for everything you do. Love ya.

Yes, it's worth it. Keep praying, leading, and influencing.

The following page includes a summary to help you pray the Seven Ps for your family.

SEVEN Ps TO PRAY
FOR MY FAMILY

1. Pray for God's peace to reign (Monday).

Pray for the peace of God, which guards, fortifies, and encompasses those who trust Him, to surround them like the mountains surround Jerusalem (Philippians 4:4-10; Psalm 125:1-2). The Bible promises that His people will live in peaceful dwellings—homes where they can experience peace (Isaiah 26:3; 32:17-18). A place for children to come to know and understand the Shalom of Jehovah. Ask God for every member of the family to know peace with God through His Son Jesus Christ.

2. Pray for the family to walk in God's purposes (Tuesday).

Pray that they will grow as fruit-bearing disciples of the Lord. Pray that they will grow in maturity in worship, discipleship, evangelism, fellowship, ministry, and the redemption of culture. May our lives be consistently marked by bearing the fruit of good character and positive influence. May each person honor the Lord and love each other.

3. Ask the Lord to fulfill His plans for your family (Wednesday).

Pray that they will know, obey, and walk in the will of God for their lives (Colossians 1:9). May the Lord help each one of us to discover our God-given bents and maximize our God-given potential. May each person mature in their unique skills, abilities, personality traits, and passions and engage in work that is fulfilling, meaningful, and profitable. May it be said of them, like King David, that they found favor in God's eyes and fulfilled their purpose in their generation. Pray for any future children, grandchildren, spouses, and descendants.

4. Pray for purity of heart, mind, and body (Thursday).

Amidst a world of impurity, pray for God's people to stay pure (Psalm 119:9-11). Pray for godliness, integrity, and moral fortitude, for the entire person to be sanctified so that they may know, reflect, and experience God (Matthew 5:8). Ask God to grow the members in wisdom, for the acquiring of discipline, understanding, prudence, knowledge, discretion, and success in relationships, life, work, and impact.

5. Ask God for His provision (Friday).

Ask the Lord to provide for the family materially (Matthew 6:11). Ask Him to provide the relationships, opportunities, and environment needed for the health, maturation, and development of the family (Psalm 24:1; Matthew 7:7-11).

6. Ask the Lord to make His presence known in the family (Saturday).

Pray for God to abundantly bless to overflowing the life, health, witness, and resources of the family. Pray for them to prosper in every way in their lives. Ask God to sovereignly cause them to supernaturally produce more than would be naturally possible. (Mt. 14:19; 2 Chron. 26:5; Ps. 118:25; 3 Jn 2; Is. 51:2). Ask God for an outpouring of the Spirit of God (Joel 2:28-29) upon your sons and daughters, resulting in the magnification and manifestation of the Lord in their lives—and that it will continue for many generations.

7. Pray for God's protection from evil (Sunday).

Pray for safety for your family members and for angels to guard them in all of their ways. Ask God to be your protector from Satan and his attacks and schemes, as well as from any physical, mental, emotional, or other harm (Mt. 6:13; 2 Co. 2:11). Ask the Lord for grace to adjust to life's changes and for the enablement to keep moving forward when we hit life's disappointments. Thank God for holding us in His hands, and may we honor God by trusting Him.

ABOUT THE AUTHOR

 Dr. Rhett Wilson, Sr., an award-winning freelance writer and editor, lives with his family in South Carolina. Rhett has pastored churches for more than twenty years, taught as an adjunct university professor, and worked as Senior Writer for the Billy Graham Evangelistic Association. His current freelance work includes serving as Director of Communications for Leighton Ford Ministries. He and his wife Tracey have three children. The Wilsons like playing board games, making music, exploring waterfalls, and they look forward to March Madness every year. For fun, Rhett reads legal thrillers, watches adventure movies, and listens to country and Broadway music. View his site at www.rhettwilson.org.

MORE RESOURCES

These resources and more can be found at
www.7psofprayer.com

- Learn how to dive deeper into the *7 Ps of Prayer*
- Check out Rhett's companion video course
- Learn about his podcast: *Faith, Family, and Freedom with Rhett Wilson*
- Sign up for Rhett's email newsletter
- Contact Rhett to speak at your conference or gathering

ENDNOTES

i The Complete Works of the Rev. Matthew Henry, vol. 1 (Grand Rapids, Mich.: Baker Book House, 1979), 260-261.

ii Whitney, Spiritual Disciplines within the Church (USA: Moody, 1996), 172-3.

iii John Franklin, And the Place Was Shaken: How to Lead a Powerful Prayer Meeting (Nashville, TN: B&H Publishing Group, 2005), 21.

iv https://biblehub.com/commentaries/pulpit/psalms/147.htm

v Darlene Rose, Evidence Not Seen (USA: Harper and Row, 1988), 144.

vi Ibid., 148.

vii James Dobson, Dr. Dobson Answers Your Questions (Wheaton, IL: Tyndale, 1982), 27-28.

viii Quoted in Sunshine Magazine as referenced in Frank Mead's 12,000 Religious Quotations (347.

ix Ben Fielding / Reuben Morgan, Mighty to Save lyrics © Hillsong Music Publishing Australia

x P. Nelson's Illustrated Bible Dictionary. Gen. Ed. Ronald Youngblood. Nashville, TN. Thomas Nelson. 960.

xi Ann Spangler, ed. The Names of God Bible (Grand Rapids, MI: Revell, 1995), 310-311.

xii https://www.compellingtruth.org/threshing-floor.html

xiii Eugene Peterson, A Long Obedience in the Same Direction (USA: IVP, 2000).

xiv Adrian Rogers with Steve Rogers, What Every Christian Ought to Know (USA: B and H Publishing, 2012), 148-9.

xv   Jerry Bridges, 31 Days Toward Trusting God (USA: NavPress, 2013), 75-76.

xvi   Charles Stanley, 30 Life Principles, 3.

xvii   Ramsey, Eva Mae. "One Red Rose." His Mysterious Ways. Carmel, NY: Guideposts, 1988. 82. Print.

xviii   Dale Carnegie and Associates, How to Win Friends and Influence People in the Digital Age (New York: Simon and Schuster, 2011), 70.

xix   Arthur, To Know Him By Name (Sisters, OR: Multnomah, 1995), 13.

xx   Webster's New Dictionary (New York: Merriam-Webster, 2001 ed.), 424.

xxi   Charles Stanley, The Wonderful, Spirit-Filled Life (USA: Thomas Nelson, 1992), 64.

xxii   Robert Coleman, The Master Plan of Evangelism (USA: Fleming Revell, 1995), 10.

xxiii   Charles Stanley, Courageous Faith (New York: Howard Books, 2016), 55.

xxiv   Bertha Smith, Go Home and Tell (Nashville: Broadman and Holman, 1995), 224.

xxv   Bob Briner, Roaring Lambs: A Gentle Plan to Radically Change Your World (Grand Rapids, MI: Zondervan, 1993), 31-32.

xxvi   Josh and Christi Straub, "Raising Kids in a Safe Home," HomeLife, May 2019; 12.

xxvii   As quoted by Lance Witt, Replenish, p. 131, Baker Books, 2011.

xxviii   See chapter three, "The Rewiring of Our Brains," in The Digital Invasion by Archibald Hart and Sylvia Hart Frejd.

xxix   G. K. Chesterton in Tom Ziglar's Choose to Win (Nashville, Tenn: Thomas Nelson, 2019), 120.

xxx   Devin Brown, Hobbit Lessons: A Map for Life's Unexpected Journeys, 13.

xxxi   14.

xxxii   EG, 65.

xxxiii   Gary Inrig, Hearts of Iron, Feet of Clay (Chicago: Moody Press, 1979), 90.

xxxiv   Steve Farrar, Battle Ready (Colorado Springs: David Cook, 2009), 117.

xxxv   https://www.dennisprager.com/americas-decay-is-speeding-up/?highlight=indoctrination

xxxvi   You can find helpful, academic, and scientific help defending a biblical understanding of creationism at both Creation Ministries International (www. creation.com) and Answers in Genesis (www.answersingenesis.org).

xxxvii   Dr. & Mrs. Howard Taylor, Hudson Taylor and the China Inland Mission; The Growth of a Work of God, Chapter 19

xxxviii   Inrig, 122.

xxxix   Richard Lee, ed. American Woman's Bible (Nashville, TN: Thomas Nelson, 2016), 632.

xl   Charles Swindoll, You and Your Child Bible Study Guide (USA: Insight for Living, 1977), 1-10.

xli   Dan Miller, 48 Days to the Work You Love (New York: Morgan James, 2020), 83.

xlii   Michael Novak, The Spirit of Democratic Capitalism

xliii   Kent Hughes, Disciplines of a Godly Man (Wheaton, Illinois: Crossway Books, 2001), 143.

xliv   Frank Mead, ed. 12,000 Religious Quotations (USA: Baker Books, 1989), 264.

xlv   https://www.blueletterbible.org/lexicon/g2513/esv/mgnt/0-1/

xlvi   John MacArthur, The MacArthur Study Bible (Crossway: Wheaton, Illinois, 2010) 871.

xlvii   Proverbs 4:23 NLT

xlviii   Dan Miller, 48 Days to the Work You Love Application Guide (Franklin, Tennessee: 48 Days, LLC, 2015), 86.

xlix   Ibid, 86.

l   Henry Cloud, Boundaries: When to Say Yes, How to Say No, to Take Control of Your Life (Grand Rapids, Mich.: Zondervan, 1992), 31.

li   Albert Mohler, https://news.sbts.edu/2006/10/05/the-lords-day-must-be-devoted-to-worship-mohler-says-in-ten-commandments-series/, accessed 03/27/2023

lii   Henry and Richard Blackaby, Experiencing God: Knowing and Doing the Will of God, Eight printing (Nashville, Tenn.: Lifeway Church Resources, 2007), 124.

liii   Terry Akrill in It Ain't Over Till It's Over by R. T. Kendall (Lake Mary, Fla.: Charisma House, 2015), 106.

liv   Tony Evans, Pathways: From Providence to Purpose (USA: Broadman and Holman, 2019), 128.

lv Mark Batterson, The Circle Maker/Draw the Circle Compilation (Grand Rapids, MI: Zondervan, 2013), 89.

lvi Steve Farrar, Manna: When You're Out of Options, God Will Provide (Nashville, Tenn.: Nelson Books, 2016), 50.

lvii Ibid., 65.

lviii Jack Canfield, The Success Principles: How to Get from Where You Are to Where You Want to Be, Tent Anniversary Edition (USA: William Morrow, 2015), 175.

lix This list is adapted from a description of "The Wise" in Warren Wiersbe's Be Skillful: God's Guidebook to Wise Living (Colorado Springs: David Cook, 1995), 76-80.

lx https://www.liberty.edu/champion/2011/09/shifting-focus-to-prayer/

lxi https://www.markbatterson.com/vague-prayers/

lxii Jack Hayford, Manifest Presence (USA: Chosen Books, 2005), 24.

lxiii Ibid., 27,29-30.

lxiv Arthur, 42.

lxv Ibid, 48.

lxvi The book was originally released under the name The Wonderful, Spirit-Filled Life.

lxvii Charles Stanley, The Spirit-Filled Life (Nashville, Tenn.: Thomas Nelson, 2014), 72-74.

lxviii Bill Bright, His Intimate Presence (Orlando, Florida: New Life Publications, 2003), 204-205.

lxix https://www.blueletterbible.org/lexicon/h3045/kjv/wlc/0-1/, accessed 04/20/2022

lxx Ray Edwards, Permission to Prosper (New York: Morgan James, 2021), 137.

lxxi His account is found in 2 Kings 9-10 and Jeremiah 35.

lxxii E. Ray Moore and Gail Pinckney Moore, The Promise of Jonadab: building a Christian family legacy in a time of cultural decline (USA: Ambassador Int'l, 2010), 58-59.

lxxiii Elisabeth Elliot, Passion and Purity, 2nd ed. (USA: Revell, 2002), 67.

lxxiv R. E. Youngblood, ed., Nelson's New Illustrated Bible Dictionary (Nashville, Tenn.: Thomas Nelson, 1995), 1242.

lxxv David McCasland, Oswald Chambers: Abandoned to God (USA: Discovery House Books, 1993), 84.

lxxvi   Wayne Grudem, Systematic Theology, second ed. (USA: Zondervan Academic, 2020), 192.

lxxvii   Charles Stanley, Waiting on God (New York: Howard Books, 2015), 162-163.

lxxviii   "K" in John Rippin's Hymns, 1787. Accessed at https://sovereign-gracemusic.org/music/songs/how-firm-a-foundation/ on 04/20/2022.

lxxix   John Newton, Public Domain.

lxxx   Two excellent books include Bible instruction about the reality of angels as well as ample testimonies of Christians who believe they encountered the angelic. I recommend Billy Graham's Angels: Ringing Assurance that We Are Not Alone and David Jeremiah's Angels: Who They Are and How They Help--What the Bible Reveals.

lxxxi   Avery Willis and Henry Blackaby, On Mission with God: Living God's Purposes for His Glory (USA: Broadman and Holman, 2002), 39.

lxxxii   Jerry Bridges, Trusting God Even When Life Hurts (USA: NavPress, 1988), 189.

lxxxiii   Kay Arthur, To Know Him by Name (USA: Multnomah, 1995), 23,26-27.